MANSA MUSA: THE GOLDEN KING OF ANCIENT MALI

Akbarali Thobhani

Metropolitan State College of Denver
Denver, Colorado

KENDALL/HUNT PUBLISHING COMPANY
4050 Westmark Drive   Dubuque, Iowa 52002

To my family

CONTENTS

Contents

Contents

Maps

PREFACE

The history of no other continent has been as much maligned or disrespected as the history of Africa, particularly the history of sub-Saharan Black Africa. Literature abounds with examples of writers over the centuries who have characterized Africans and their history in the most unflattering terms. At the worst, Africa, except for the Nile Valley, was regarded as a continent without history. Professor J. D. Fage has pointed out that Africa was completely ignored in the first *Cambridge Modern History*. These negative views continue to persist among many around the world even today as we approach the end of another millennium. However, over the last fifty years, with African countries regaining their independence from the colonial domination, the study of African history has undergone a significant transformation. A new breed of scholars, more guided by the rules of objectivity and with open minds, has come to the forefront. Unshackled by paternalistic attitudes and negative mindset, these scholars have immersed themselves into researching and uncovering the African past not only on the basis of how the outsiders imagined Africa to be, but also by studying the traditions of the native peoples themselves. The work of these scholars, both native and non-native, has resulted in demolishing many of the old and racist myths about the African past. As Philip Curtin and his colleagues state "African history has come of age." Contrary to the negative images and myths about Africa, there is much of substance and significance to learn about the Africans and their past.

Mansa Kankan Musa is one of the most renowned figures in early African history. In the annals of fourteenth century West African history, his name is associated with wealth, power, and fame. He ruled over the ancient empire of Mali during the first half of the fourteenth century. During his rule, the empire is regarded to have achieved its greatest territorial size covering a large portion of the middle region of West Africa from beyond the Niger River in the east to the Atlantic Ocean in the west and to have reached the pinnacle of its economic prosperity and military might.

The story of ancient Mali has been recounted and analyzed by numerous prominent scholars of African history. Nehemiah Levtzion, J. Spencer Trimingham, E. W. Bovill, Madina Ly Tall, D. T. Niane, Basil Davidson, R. Mauny, Charles

Monteil, M. Delafosse are some of the leading modern scholars who have shed much light on the history of ancient Mali. Their research, recording of oral traditions, translations and critical analyses of ancient sources which are primarily in the Arabic language, have contributed much to our knowledge and understanding of the history of ancient Mali. Their work has revealed to us the details about the pomp; the lifestyles; and the political, economic, military and diplomatic characteristics of ancient West African states as remembered by *griots*, the oral historians, and as recorded by Arabic/Islamic authors whose writings provide the earliest recorded descriptions and testimonies about the Sudanic states of West Africa. The present work is greatly indebted to the work of these and numerous other authors.

The present effort is undertaken primarily to underscore for and to provide to my students of African history in particular and interested general readers a more substantial, in-depth and current description of the life and times of a major African ruler of a renowned African empire than is possible within the limits of two or three fast-paced lectures. Economic, religious, political and military factors that contributed to the rise of ancient Mali and that enabled Mansa Musa to reign over one of the largest states on the African continent are examined in some detail. The author of this work will seek to synthesize available information about Mansa Musa in particular. While ancient sources, whether oral or written, are extremely valuable, they are not without problems. They are sometimes very brief and fragmentary; they mention and describe places that have vanished or have not yet been positively identified; they are sometimes inconsistent and contradictory; they are sometimes based on hearsay; they sometimes contain irrational and incredible tales; and for the period prior to 1500, they are written by outsiders, mainly Arab and Berber natives of Spain, North Africa or even beyond. Thus, the modern scholars confront numerous challenges as they attempt to piece together the histories of early West African states and societies. These issues along with points of agreement and disagreement among modern scholars regarding some aspects of the ancient history of Mali and Mansa Musa will be presented.

The present day Republic of Mali, much of which formed part of the ancient empire of Mali, is among the economically poorest countries of the world. The people of modern Mali are suffering from poverty, unemployment and numerous other socio-economic problems associated with modernization. However, within its borders are located traditions, artifacts, and places that are of immense historical value. The memory and legacy of ancient Mali is very much alive in modern Mali and in the neighboring countries of Guinea and Gambia.

My thanks and gratitude are owed to several colleagues at The Metropolitan State College of Denver who offered much support and encouragement towards the completion of the present work. In particular, I wish to mention Dr. C. J. White, Chairperson of the African American Studies Department, whose professional friendship and advise has been greatly valued. And to my wife Taz, who not only provided much encouragement but also helped with translation of some Arabic passages. Finally to the Kendall/Hunt Publishing Company for their enthusiastic acceptance of this work for publication.

Africa: Modern Day Countries

CHAPTER 1

RISE OF ANCIENT MALI

Introduction

The earliest and most prolific written sources about the peoples and states of the Western Sudan south of the Sahara, especially for the period before 1500, have come to us from the pens of Arab and Berber Muslim writers from North Africa, Spain, Syria and a few even from the Iranian Muslim chroniclers. These writers, and in general the Arabic-speaking world, referred to Africa south of the Sahara as *Bilad as-Sudan* (the country of the Black Peoples). Thus, there was Eastern Sudan which included Nubia and Ethiopia, and there was Western Sudan which included the lands to the south of the Sahara and the north of the forest belt of modern West Africa. Texts and chronicles written by West Africans themselves began to appear mostly after 1500, and due to the Islamization that had occurred by then, these sources, as are the others, are in the Arabic language. After the exploration of the West African coastline by the Portuguese from the mid-1400s, European accounts become increasingly important. However, by this time, the ancient empire of Mali had passed its golden age and had significantly declined; therefore, these primary European sources are valuable for the later history of West Africa. During the last 100 to 150 years, from approximately the 1850s to the present, European, American and other foreign scholars have played a major part by uncovering, translating and publishing many of these ancient sources. While Africans were enduring the brutalities of the slave trade and colonialism, many foreign explorers, scholars and researchers were revealing anew to the rest of the world the glories of ancient Africa as recorded by the early historians and chroniclers. At the time when the first Arabic accounts about the Western Sudan were written in the ninth century, the ancient empire of Ghana was one of the handful of African states known to the outsiders. It was considered to be the wealthiest and the most powerful of the states in the Western Sudan. Its fame was due to the production and trade in gold. It was also known for its military might. Its fame had reached as far as Mesopotamia to the east and

Muslim Spain to the north. The first reference to Ghana in the Arabic sources dates back to the late eighth century in the writing of Al-Fazari (Levtzion & Hopkins, 1981). During the ninth and the tenth centuries, numerous other writers made references to Ghana almost always mentioning its gold. A Spanish Muslim writer of the eleventh century, Al-Bakri, provided the first in-depth description of some aspects of the life and culture of Ghana. Based upon information gathered from individuals who had traveled to Ghana and whom he had met in Spain, Al-Bakri wrote about the economy and some of the customs and provided descriptions of some of the towns of ancient Ghana.

During the second half of the eleventh century, lands to the north and northwest of ancient Ghana witnessed the emergence of a very powerful and militant Islamic movement founded by Abd Allah ibn Yasin and known as the Almoravids. This movement, as it grew in strength and surged out throughout the Maghreb (North-west Africa), was to have a major impact upon the histories of Northwest Africa, Spain and the Western Sudan. The Almoravid movement and its expansion through military conquests became one of the major reasons for the collapse of ancient Ghana's power. In the 1060s, the Almoravid army reached the territory of ancient Ghana and dealt it a heavy blow. In the aftermath of the Almoravid conquest, ancient Ghana and its people, the Soninke, continued to exist but in a much weakened state. Decades later, the Soso people, a Western Sudanese people, under their leader Sumanguru rose in the region and conquered numerous states including ancient Ghana. Subsequently, a struggle ensued between the people who founded the empire of ancient Mali and the Soso which resulted in the defeat of Sumanguru and the Soso. This struggle is taken up in more detail below.

The first written reference to Mali is believed to have been made by Al-Bakri in his book *Kitab al-masalik wa-'l-mamalik* ("The Book of Routes and Realms," 1068) where he refers to a country called Malal (Levtzion & Hopkins, 1981). During the next few centuries, from the twelfth to the fourteenth, only sporadic references to Malal or Mali appear in records. Therefore, in these first records, hardly anything is included regarding the rise of ancient Mali into prominence. It is not until the fourteenth century that writers leave us more detailed descriptions on various aspects of the people and culture of ancient Mali. Among the most prominent of these fourteenth century authors in connection with the history of Mali are Al-Umari (1301-1349), Ibn Battuta (1304-1368), and Ibn Khaldun (1332-1406). The writings of these individuals are extremely important and they will be referred to throughout this work.

Before proceeding further in exploring the rise of ancient Mali, it is worthwhile to note that many of these early Arab writers had incorporated information from the writings of Greek scholars, particularly "facts" and frameworks relating to geographical descriptions of the known world at the time. Also, it appears that the Arab writers had been influenced by the Judeo-Christian tradition regarding the story of Ham and the curse, for we find a number of these Arab writers describing the black African peoples of the Eastern and Western Sudan as descendants of various sons of Ham and being afflicted by Noah's curse on Ham. The Quran, while containing verses about Noah, does not mention the curse. The curse, according to the Judeo-Christian traditions, was placed by Noah upon the descendants of one of his sons, Ham, because of a transgression committed by Ham against his father. The original curse condemned some of the descendants of Ham to be servants to the rest. However, in later theological elaborations of the curse, the black color of a person came to be regarded as a symbol of the curse. Thus, black Africans were identified as a race of people that had descended from Ham.

Emergence of Mali

For information about the early rise of Mali, our primary sources are the numerous oral traditions that have been preserved by the people. Oral tradition, despite its shortcomings, has increasingly come to be recognized and valued as an important source for understanding the African past. Oral traditions that trace and explain the circumstances and events surrounding the origin of Mali some eight centuries ago are still recounted and celebrated up to the present time. Even though these stories contain some fantastic and incredible details and may be more legendary than factual, they are our only clues to the beginning chapters of the history of ancient Mali.

Ancient Mali originated in the region of the upper Niger River in the savanna belt of West Africa. To the south lay the forest region and the coast, and to the north lay the massive Sahara Desert. Ancient Mali was associated with the Malinke people of West Africa. They are one of the peoples who belong to the Mande language group. This is one of the sub-groups within the larger Niger-Kordofanian language group, one of the four major language groups into which peoples and languages of Africa are generally classified. The people associated with ancient Ghana, the Soninke, are also a part of this Mande sub-group. The Mande-speaking peoples have generally occupied the region that in today's map of West Africa would include southern Mali, northern Guinea, eastern Senegal, and northwestern Ivory Coast.

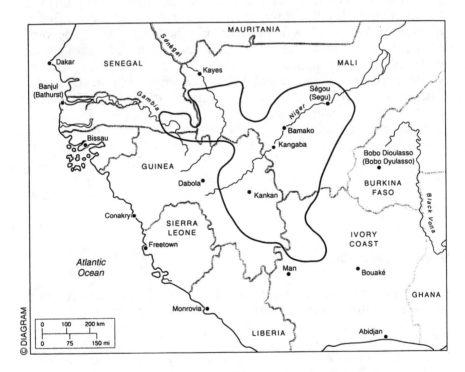

Distribution of Malinke People

    The Malinke, like many other pre-literate peoples of the world, preserved their history and traditions through memorization and passed their history and traditions down to the future generations by word of mouth. Specialists existed in these cultures whose primary responsibilities were to keep the past alive. These oral traditionalists or *griots* were found at the level of family, village, clan, and the royal palace. They served as counselors, tutors, musicians, constitutionalists, and intermediaries in the palace. As Madina Ly Tall points out in his book *L'Empire du*

Mali (1977) the *griot* was a person of great importance in the royal court of Mali.

The struggle between the Malinke of Mali and the Soso, described in detail below, marked a major turning point in the history of ancient Mali. It resulted in the transformation of Mali from a minor state to an imperial power. Prior to this struggle in the 1230s, tradition says that there were sixteen kings of Mali (Niane, 1965) who had descended from Bilal, the first *muezzin* (prayer caller) of Islam and a companion of the Prophet Muhammad (May Peace Be Upon Him). As per this tradition, one of the seven sons of Bilal named Lowalo left Mecca and settled in Mali. Succeeding Lowalo were Latal Kabali, Damul Kabali, and Lahilatul Kabali. According to Al-Bakri, Islam is said to have reached Mali (Malal) during the eleventh century. One of the later sources, Ibn Khaldun, mentions that King Baramandana was the first Malian king to have accepted Islam in the 1050s. The other rulers of Mali during the pre-empire period are identified as Hamana, Djigui Bilali, Musa Keita or Allakoi, and Nare Famaghan (Ki-Zerbo, 1978). There are differences of opinion among modern scholars regarding these early rulers' conversions to Islam. These are explored in a later chapter.

The story of the great struggle between the Malinke and the Soso which then led to the origin of the empire of Mali is remembered and told by the Malinke *griots* in several different versions. Johnson (1992) identifies over a dozen versions of this epic that are now in print. While these versions differ in some important details, they concur on the basic themes and the nature of the struggle between the Soso and the Malinke, and the outcome of this struggle. The most widely referenced oral tradition about this early period is contained in D. T. Niane's *SUNDIATA: An Epic of Old Mali* (translated from the original in French by G. D. Picket, 1965). The author of this work, Niane, is recognized as a leading scholar on the traditional interpretations of the history of ancient Mali. Another version is contained in Roland Bertol's *SUNDIATA: The Epic of the Lion King* (1977). The Sundiata story is a most famous one and quite central in the mythology of Mali and, therefore, the essential highlights of this story are summarized here based upon the Niane and Bertol versions.

The Sundiata Story

The epic of Sundiata contains elements of high drama, references to the practice of sorcery, the ideas of destiny, intra-familial rivalry and jealousy, a touch of incest and cruelty, and finally the triumph of good over evil. The story takes place among the Keita clan of the Malinke. It begins when Nare Maghan was the king of the Keita clan and ruled from the town of Niani. He was the father of numerous sons (3 or 11 according to different versions) and several daughters. Nare Maghan was, on one occasion, visited by a stranger who was a hunter and a diviner. After this hunter-diviner was warmly welcomed by King Nare Maghan, he prophesied that the King's successor was yet to be born. He continued that the King would one day be visited by two other hunters accompanied by a woman from the kingdom of Do. However, this woman would be very ugly with a humped back. The diviner told the King that this is the woman he must marry, for she will bear him the son who would bring power and immortality to Mali. The son, said the diviner, "will be more mighty than Alexander (the Great)" (Niane, 1965). After conveying this prophecy, the diviner left the court and the town of Niani.

Sometime later, the two hunters and the ugly woman did arrive in the town of Niani as prophesied. The woman was named Sogolon Kedjou. Recalling the prophecy, the king, Nare Maghan, decided to marry her. Elaborate preparations were made and dignitaries from many nearby states came to the wedding. She became the second wife of the King, the first one being Sassouma Berete. Soon after the wedding, Sogolon became pregnant and gave birth to a son who was named Mari Djata. He also became variously known as Sundiata, Sunjara or Sun Djata. At this point, the first wife, Sassouma, who was not happy to begin with, became very concerned that this newborn son could deprive her own son's right to succeed to the throne.

It is said that Sundiata was even more ugly than his mother. He was born with a large head, large eyes, and, worst of all, he was unable to stand up on his feet and walk. He was a crawling baby. The boy's physical shortcomings made a mockery of the prophecy that he would be the great conqueror. Even King Nare Maghan became disillusioned and no longer maintained any faith in the prophecy. These were difficult days for Sologon, the mother. She bore another child for the King but this time it was a daughter. According to the tradition, the only person who rejoiced from this state of affairs was the King's first wife, Sassouma. She

6

teased and joked about Sundiata's unhealthy physical condition at every opportunity and with pleasure too. Sundiata was still crawling at age seven. Ultimately, when the time came for the King to designate his successor, he chose Dankara Touman, the son of his first wife. Upon the king's death, the first wife became even more nasty towards Sogolon and Sundiata. But, as fate would have it, sometime during the child's seventh year, in reaction to another one of Sassouma's insults, the child gathered enough strength to stand upright and walked for the first time much to the joy of his mother. She felt that God had finally heard her prayer.

Sundiata then joined the rest of the community as a normal child. The "miracle" made him a popular child. He began to make up for lost time and became rapidly acculturated into the Keita traditions—hunting, playing, learning about plants and animals and other local activities. And, due to the fact that he was a royal child, he was instructed in the history of the ancient kings.

As Sundiata's strength and popularity continued to increase, those elders who were familiar with the prophecy of the diviner became more convinced and believed that Sundiata was destined to be a great king. Sassouma, the first wife, did not find any comfort in this changed condition of Sundiata, especially since she regarded her own son, Dankara Touman, who was the ruling king, as a weak ruler and was fearful that he could easily be replaced. Therefore, she began to think about permanently eliminating the possibility of Sundiata replacing her son on the throne. The first wife concluded in her mind that Sundiata must be killed. She brought a few witches into the plot and a plan was worked out. However, the plan failed and the witches switched sides and revealed the details of the conspiracy to Sundiata. Sogolon, Sundiata's mother, no longer felt secure staying in the palace and decided when Sundiata was eleven years old to take the family to a distant but more safe and friendly environment. Thus, the exile. The family, consisting of Sundiata, his mother, his sister, and a half brother, left the palace of Niani much to the pleasure of Sassouma, the first wife. They walked for days and months. They sought refuge in several states. They went to Djedeba, Tabon and Ghana-Wagadu. In each of these places they received generally warm but only temporary hospitality. Ultimately, they arrived at the court of the king of Mema, a nearby country to the north. The king of Mema, who at that time was Moussa Tounkara, treated the royal refugees from Niani well. He took in Sundiata as his own son. He took him on military campaigns and gave him experiences in other matters of governing a kingdom. Sogolon was very happy.

She had removed Sundiata from harm's way. She believed that Sundiata was destined to return to his home kingdom and play a major role in the history of the Malinke. So, for several years she and her children enjoyed the friendship of the royal family of Mema.

In the meantime, the history of the region was being impacted by other key players and the region was undergoing a major upheaval. The ancient empire of Ghana had been delivered a powerful blow by the Almoravid movement towards the end of the eleventh century. Founded by Abd Allah ibn Yasin in the middle of the eleventh century, the Almoravid movement was a reformist Muslim movement that had gained so much strength that it militarily overthrew a number of Islamic dynasties in Morocco and Spain during the second half of the eleventh century. One wing of the Almoravid movement had struck southwards from its base in the Moroccan and Mauritanian region. The empire of Ghana never fully recovered from that invasion, and although it continued to exist, it was in a much weakened state. Thus there was somewhat of a power vacuum in the region. In the early 1200s, the Soso people embarked on the process of creating an empire under their domination that would take the place of ancient Ghana. Sumanguru (also referred to as Soumaoro) was the great king of the Soso who had launched this effort. Sumanguru was quite successful. His army had conquered several kingdoms including the ancient kingdom of Ghana. Numerous Malinke chiefdoms came under the domination of Sumanguru between 1200 and 1230.

Sumanguru is portrayed in the Malinke traditions as a villain. He was a brutal conqueror. His rule was harsh and the peoples that his army conquered felt terrorized. Additionally, Sumanguru was regarded as a sorcerer king. He made use of magic to remain in power and defeat his enemies. His residence, built like a tower, is reputed to have had a secret chamber where he kept the skulls and skins of his vanquished enemy rulers. Fear and terror were the hallmarks of Sumanguru's reign for the non-Soso people. The Keita kingdom centered around the town of Niani was also conquered by Sumanguru. Sundiata's half brother, Dankara Touman, who had succeeded Sundiata's father to the throne and was the ruler of Niani when Sundiata and his family went into exile, was still the ruler of Niani at the time of its conquest by Sumanguru. After Sumanguru's conquest of Niani, Dankara Touman remained in power for a while but as a humiliated and a subjugated chief. He eventually fled.

In the course of time, Sumanguru's army ravaged the town of Niani. It was looted and pillaged, and its inhabitants were cruelly treated. Sumanguru "was an evil demon and his reign had produced nothing but bloodshed," recalled the *griot* Djeli Mamoudou Kouyate (Niane, 1965). The Keita people lamented. This was the worst period in their existence. They had joined other victims of Sumanguru's empire. Some of their women were forced into marriages with the Soso conquerors, including a half sister of Sundiata whom Sumanguru himself took as a wife. Some of the administrators of Niani were forced to serve the new masters. Who could rescue them from this terrible fate? Some had remembered the old prophecy made by the diviner. The son of the former King Nare Maghan and the ugly wife (Sogolon) would be the Keita's great conqueror. But Sundiata had been gone for some years. His exact whereabouts were not known to the people of his home town of Niani.

A search party was sent to scout the nearby states to locate Sundiata. Within several months, the efforts of the search party were successful. Sundiata was located in the kingdom of Mema where he had grown to be a mature young man with the reputation of a brave person. Sundiata was given all the horrible details about the conquest of Niani by Sumanguru and the suffering of his people. The messengers urged him that it was time for him to end his exile and return to lead the Malinke people against Sumanguru and liberate their homeland. Sundiata saw no choice but to respond positively to the plea and he made preparations to return and wage a war of liberation. He took leave of his host, King Moussa Tounkara of Mema. However, before Sundiata left Mema, his mother Sogolon died and he buried her in Mema. In order to assist Sundiata in his upcoming struggle with Sumanguru, the King of Mema transferred a portion of his own army to Sundiata for his upcoming war.

As Sundiata and his army marched towards a confrontation with the "evil" Sumanguru, he traversed through several other kingdoms, some of whose kings also contributed warriors to Sundiata. The king of Wagadu is said to have given half of his army to Sundiata. Thus, Sundiata had successfully forged a grand alliance of Malinke and other groups who wanted to see an end to Sumanguru's tyranny. The alliance had also attracted the hated Sumanguru's own nephew whose young bride was violated by Sumanguru. The struggle to vanquish Sumanguru had taken on mythological dimensions. It was a struggle between good and evil.

It was a struggle that was destined. It was a struggle that would test a prophecy.

Soon, the two armies engaged in combat. Several preliminary victories by Sundiata's forces set the stage for the final showdown in Krina. Krina is just south of the city of Bamako, the capital of present-day Mali. Prior to the Battle of Krina, as the war of liberation was unfolding, another interesting secret aspect about Sumanguru was revealed to Sundiata. Sumanguru, being a sorcerer king and a practitioner of magic, had a weakness. The antidote to his magical powers was a 'rooster's spur.' Sundiata's half sister, who had been forcefully taken as a wife by Sumanguru after the conquest of Niani, had uncovered this secret. She had managed to escape from Sumanguru and had joined up with Sundiata. Bertol's (1977) narrative provides a different version on how this secret was obtained and, according to this version, it was Sundiata's childhood *griot* who had been forced into the service of the 'evil' Sumanguru who tricked Sumanguru into revealing the secret. Anyway, at the showdown in Krina, Sundiata was prepared to use the antidote.

The Battle of Krina is generally regarded to have occurred around 1235. As the battle raged, Sundiata sought out Sumanguru and fired off his arrow that was tinged with the "rooster's spur." It hit Sumanguru on the shoulder. The sorcerer king fled according to one version. Sumanguru was no more. The epic battle had been won. Soso was destroyed. As the *griot* narrated, "The victory of Krina was dazzling. The remains of Soumaoro's (Sumanguru's) army went to shut themselves up in Sosso (sic). But the empire of the Sosso was done for. From everywhere around kings sent their submission to Sundiata. The king of Guiinakhan sent a richly furnished embassy to Djata (one of the several different versions of Sundiata's name) and at the same time gave his daughter in marriage to the victor" (Niane, 1965).

Sundiata's triumph at Krina resulted in important political ramifications for the Malinke clans that were allied in the struggle. Important rules that governed relationships among the Malinke clans were established there. New political and constitutional customs that remained part of the Malinke culture for a long time were initiated in the aftermath of the victory. These, according to the traditions, were as follows: Sundiata was proclaimed as the supreme Mansa (King) of the Malinke; future kings of the Malinke must be from the line of Sundiata; princes are obligated to always select their first wife from the clan of Sundiata's mother; certain clans are designated as guardians of the faith; and clans were established that corresponded with the practicing of particular trades and crafts, thus making the practice of these trades and crafts a matter of heredity (Niane, 1984). The component states of the empire were classified into two categories. Those that had been the original allies of Sundiata were allowed to be ruled by their own kings with their own titles, whereas the rest were subjected to the presence of a governor from Sundiata.

Before returning to Niani, Sundiata had conquered the Soso-dominated lands and went beyond. Numerous nearby territories such as Diaghan, Bambougou, Fouta, and Kita, which were all former allies of Sumanguru, were all conquered (Niane, 1965). At a grand assembly in the Malinke state of Kangaba, Sundiata was proclaimed the supreme Mansa (King). Finally, according to the Niane version, he returned to Niani, his birthplace, and rebuilt the town which served as one of the capitals of the empire of Mali. Sundiata is also said to have converted his victorious army into a standing professional force ready to defend as well as expand the territory of the liberated state (Shinnie, 1965). Also, Sundiata attached much importance to the enhancement of agricultural production in the new empire both for making the new empire self-sufficient in food as well as for increasing trade (Chu and Skinner, 1965).

As pointed out earlier, there are different versions of this epic among the various Malinke clans. One important difference between the oral tradition as contained in the Niane version and that presented by Bertol concerns the presence of Islamic influence among the Keita of Niani during the pre-Sundiata period. The subject of the spread of the Islamic presence and influence in ancient Mali and the Western Sudan is taken up in a later chapter of this work. Suffice it to state here that the version presented by Bertol reflects a much more significant presence of Islam among the Malinke in the early phase of the history of Mali between the eleventh and the middle of the thirteenth centuries. Another important difference is that before Sundiata had left for the exile, the 'evil' Sumanguru had killed eleven brothers and half brothers of Sundiata, each one of whom had succeeded to the throne of Niani and challenged Sumanguru. Sundiata was spared by Sumanguru because of his sickly condition.

Both of the above versions of the Sundiata epic as presented by D. T. Niane and Bertol closely associate the town of Niani with Sundiata. These versions strongly suggest that the town of Niani was the birthplace of Sundiata and that it was from this town that he departed for the exile with his mother and family.

And, after his victory over Sumanguru at the battle of Krina around 1235, according to D. T. Niane's version, Sundiata returned to his place of birth, Niani, and established it as the seat of the government of Mali. He is said to have rebuilt the town, and many people from surrounding villages came and settled there. Tranquillity, happiness and prosperity prevailed in Niani under Sundiata. However, there exist significant differences of opinion among other traditionalists in Mali and among modern scholars regarding the location of Sundiata's seat of power and government. David Conrad in a 1994 article on the subject provides an excellent review of the controversy and the differences of opinion regarding the ancient capital of Mali. According to Conrad, an examination of numerous other oral versions of the Sundiata epic and the available archaeological and textual materials led him to conclude that Niani was not the town in which Sundiata spent his pre-exile years, nor was it the town used by Sundiata as his capital after his rise to power. Instead, he concludes, the evidence points to the town of Dakajalan as Sundiata's birthplace and the town to which he returned after his victory. The town of Dakajalan is located much further to the north along the main portion of the Niger River, while Niani is located near the border between modern Mali and Guinea to the south and along Sankarani, a tributary of the Niger River. So, for the moment, there is no consensus on the exact location of the imperial seat of power of the nascent empire of Mali in the thirteenth century at the dawn of its emergence. Niane suggests that during the pre-Sundiata period, Dakajalan (or Dakadiala as he calls it) was used by several kings as their place of residence, but Sundiata chose to move to Niani because it afforded a more secure environment and also because it was closer to the sources of gold and valuable agricultural goods that came from the forest region (Niane, 1984). Controversy also exists with regard to the location of ancient Mali's capital in the fourteenth century during the peak of its power. This will be discussed in a later chapter.

Fourteenth Century Arabic Accounts of Mali

Following the period of Sundiata and the establishment of the empire of Mali, there are more frequent and detailed written accounts about ancient Mali that appeared in the writings of Arab and Berber authors of the fourteenth century. As mentioned earlier, the most important of these accounts were penned by Al-Umari

(1301-49), Ibn Battuta (1304-68), and Ibn Khaldun (1332-1406). These are extremely important writers and their accounts are referred to extensively throughout this work; therefore, some background information about each one of them and the circumstances of their acquaintances with the land, the people and the history of ancient Mali are summarized below. For information provided below and translations of these authors' writings from Arabic, the present author has greatly relied on the work of N. Levtzion and J. F. P. Hopkins, *Corpus of Early Arabic Sources for West African History* (1981).

Al-Umari was a native of Damascus, Syria, where he was born in 1301. However, his family had relocated and lived in Cairo for some years where his father served in a senior capacity in the administration of the Mamluk rulers of Egypt. One of his major works, titled "Pathways of Vision in the Realms of the Metropolises," contains important information about ancient Mali (Levtzion & Hopkins, 1981). Al-Umari never visited Mali. He gathered his knowledge from individuals who had resided in Mali or had traveled to trade in Mali and from Egyptian officials who had met with and known Mansa Musa. Al-Umari died in Damascus in 1349.

The second major author, Ibn Battuta, was the only one of the three who had actually traveled to ancient Mali. Ibn Battuta is acknowledged as one of the greatest adventurers and travelers in the history of the world. He even surpassed Marco Polo in the duration and distance covered, as well as the number of countries to which he traveled. Ibn Battuta was born in Tangier, Morocco in 1304. In 1324, a year after Marco Polo's death, as a devout Muslim, he left his home to go on a *hajj* (pilgrimage) to Mecca. This journey turned into a 24-year-long tour through much of the Islamic world in North Africa, the Middle East, Central Asian Republics, the Indian sub-continent, and the Swahili city states along East Africa. He even traveled to Russia and China. Along the way he performed several pilgrimages in Mecca. In 1352, he embarked on his last journey which was to traverse the Sahara Desert to Western Sudan. He traveled and sojourned in ancient Mali for nearly two years. Upon his return to his homeland, the Sultan of Morocco provided a scribe, Ibn Juzzay, to record the account of these travels as dictated by Ibn Battuta. The work was completed in 1355. Ibn Battuta died in 1368 in the city of Marrakech, founded by the Almoravids (the conquerors of ancient Ghana) in the eleventh century. He is recognized by many scholars as the greatest of all travelers. The "Rihla," as the work has come to be known, provides us with the first eye-witness account about Mali by a visitor. For medieval African history, his work is regarded as the best, the most extensive and reliable. According to the *New Encyclopedia Britannica* (vol. 6, 1995), "The documentary value of his work has given it lasting historical and geographical significance."

Our third major author, Ibn Khaldun, was born in Tunis in 1332. Ibn Khaldun is the most renowned of all Arab historians. Most of his life was spent in the employ of North African rulers. He ended up living in Cairo where he died in 1406. Ibn Khaldun is regarded as one of the intellectual giants, a jewel of the Islamic civilization. His book *Kitab al-Ibar* is a major work on the history of the Arabs, the Persians and the Berbers (Levtzion and Hopkins, 1981). He was quite cognizant of the important ties between the Western Sudan and the countries to the north of the Sahara. He also obtained his information about Mali from native residents of Mali and other travelers.

Apart from the above three, there are a few other Arab authors whose writings contain anecdotal references and descriptions about ancient Mali or its rulers. These will be cited as appropriate.

The above-described story of Sundiata and Sumanguru, while so important in the oral traditions, is referenced in the early Arabic written records by only one of these authors. Ibn Khaldun, who had learned about it from one of his informants who had lived in Mali, briefly mentions the conquest of Soso by Mali (Levtzion & Hopkins, 1981).

West African Accounts

From the sixteenth and the seventeenth centuries, we get our first written accounts about ancient Mali from the native West Africans themselves. By the sixteenth century, important and renowned centers of learning and scholarship had developed in several Western Sudanese cities such as Timbuktu, Gao, and Jenne which attracted Arab, Berber and West African scholars. Leo Africanus, who was born into a Muslim family in Spain and then lived in Morocco, visited Timbuktu in the early 1500s and observed the following in his famous book, the *History and Description of Africa*. In Timbuktu "there is a great store of doctors, judges, priests, and other learned men, that are bountifully maintained at the king's costs and charges. And hither are brought diuers manuscripts or written bookes out of Barbarie, which are sold for more money than any other merchandise" (John Pory's translation 1600, edited by Robert Brown, 1896). Leo Africanus' book, which was completed in 1526, gave Europe the first detailed account of the interior of Africa. His book was a treasure chest of information and for two and a half centuries it was regarded as indispensable by all who were interested in Africa. More background about him and his observations about ancient Mali are described in a later chapter. Suffice it to state here that Leo Africanus was greatly impressed with the scholarly and intellectual community of Timbuktu in the early 1500s. Timbuktu enjoyed its golden age during the sixteenth century.

While these West African native records are from the post-Mali period, they nonetheless are valuable because they give us insights into what the Western Sudanese knew, thought and wrote about ancient Mali. Two of the most significant of these sources are *Tarikh as-Sudan* by Abderahman as-Sadi and *Tarikh al-Fattash* by Mahmud Kati. (These have been translated from Arabic into French by O. Houdas.) As-Sadi was born in Timbuktu in 1596 when the empire of Songhay, the successor empire to Mali, was entering its declining years. The bulk of As-Sadi's work is devoted to the history of Songhay, but it does contain a chapter on Mansa Musa and a very brief chapter on the kingdom of Mali. Mahmud Kati was also born in Timbuktu in 1468 and is said to have lived over a hundred years. He was a prominent *qadi* (Muslim judge) in Timbuktu and is said to have accompanied Askiya Mohammad Toure, the famous sixteenth century ruler of Songhay, on a pilgrimage to Mecca. Other members of his family are also said to have contributed to this work.

Following Sundiata's victory, Mali replaced ancient Ghana in prominence, power, wealth and fame. The war of liberation from the domination of the Soso had evolved into an expansionist one. Sundiata consolidated the newly regained independence and went on to add to the size of his domain through his own conquests further west and north. In fact, Mali became several times larger in size than ancient Ghana. It extended from the region of the Upper Niger all the way to the Atlantic. Rich gold fields were also conquered. Mali became a successor to Ghana as the leading commercial and military power of Western Sudan.

Succession of Rulers in Ancient Mali

While there are uncertainties about the number and names of the rulers of ancient Mali in the pre-Sundiata period, the post-Sundiata picture is much clearer. Ibn Khaldun has left us with a fairly complete genealogy of the ruling dynasty of Mali from the reign of Sundiata until the end of the fourteenth century. Sundiata is said to have ruled for twenty five-years until 1255. How death came to Sundiata is uncertain. One tradition mentions an accidental wound from a weapon as the cause of his death, while another states that he drowned in the Sankarani River, a tributary of the Niger River. According to Niane, Sundiata was buried near the place where he drowned and his tomb is still located there (1965). Circumstances that led to his drowning, if that was the cause, are unknown. There are many villages in Mali today that continue to commemorate the life of Sundiata through recounting the epic of Sundiata, and having ceremonies of sacrifices and performances of music and drama (Niane, 1984).

Ancient Mali's prosperity, power and fame were, in part, due to two significant factors—its control of the numerous southern termini of the trans-Saharan trade and its acceptance of Islam. Both of these subjects are taken up in detail in other chapters. These factors gave Mali and other states of the Western Sudan in a similar category a prominent place on the stage of world history. Its Islamic character drew the attention and focus of traders, travelers, scholars and sultans of other Muslim states. Despite the vastness and the harshness of the Sahara Desert, Western Sudan was linked to a major part of the Islamic world in a symbiotic relationship driven by trade and a shared faith.

In the decades following Sundiata's death to the ascendancy to power of Mansa Musa, Mali was ruled by six different kings. Based upon information from Ibn Khaldun, a chronology of these kings has been developed by modern scholars, most notably by Delafosse. However, minor variations are commonly found in the dates given by different authors for each of these kings. Sundiata was succeeded by his eldest son Mansa Uli. Mansa Uli ruled from 1255 to 1270. Ibn Khaldun described him as "one of their greatest kings" (Levtzion & Hopkins, 1981). However, considering that he ruled for about fifteen years and made a pilgrimage to Mecca, not much is recorded or known about him. He is said to have continued the policy of expansion. Joseph Ki-Zerbo, a prominent West African historian, in his work *Histoire de l'Afrique Noire* (1978), suggests that at this time some decentralization occurred in the empire along the feudatory model. D.T.Niane, the author of *SUNDIATA: An Epic of Mali* and numerous other studies on the Western Sudanese history, suggests that Mansa Uli's coming to power marked a rupture in the traditional pattern of succession which was fratrilineal. Niane further suggests that the kingship was forcibly taken by Uli and that it was perhaps during his reign that the Malinke conquered and settled in the territories in the region of the Senegal and Gambia rivers (1984).

Following Mansa Uli's death, the empire experienced some turbulent times. The empire almost disintegrated during the reigns of the next several rulers (Niane, 1984). Dynastic conflicts, rebellions and maladministration are said to have characterized the political history of the empire over the next decade. Mansa Uli was succeeded by his brother Mansa Wati who ruled for only four years (1270-74). The sources are quite silent about his rule. Only his name and the dates of his reign are mentioned. It is important to note that succession passed along fratrilineal lines conforming with the local customs. The throne then passed to Mansa Khalifa, another brother of Mansa Uli. Thus, there were three brothers in a row to rule the empire. Mansa Khalifa's rule was the shortest, only one year. Ibn Khaldun informs us that Khalifa was mentally deranged. His quick downfall is attributed to his habit of entertaining himself by senselessly causing death of some of his subjects by shooting arrows at them (Levtzion & Hopkins, 1981). The people revolted against him and killed him.

Following Mansa Khalifa's death, the line of succession went in another interesting direction. The next Mansa who came to power was the son of Sundiata's daughter. He was named Abu Bakr. Thus, the three brothers were succeeded by a nephew. (This pattern of succession has been and continues to be practiced by a number of cultures in West Africa. Today, the most famous of the West African peoples who practice this type of succession are the Ashanti people of modern Ghana.) the 11th century author Al-Bakri wrote that this pattern of succession was also common among the Soninke of ancient Ghana. He recounted that the kingship was passed only through the son of the king's sister. The reason, he explained, was that the people never had any doubt about who the mother of the son was, whereas doubts could exist about a father-son relationship (Levtzion & Hopkins, 1981).

Mansa Abu Bakr is said to have ruled for about ten years until 1285. Levtzion suggests that Abu Bakr was favored by the officers of the court because, perhaps, they saw him to be more amenable to their influences (Levtzion, 1963). There seems to be some confusion about the beginning date of his reign. The chronology developed by Charles Monteil (cited in Levtzion, 1963) and also used by Niane (1984) shows the first two years of Abu Bakr's reign overlapping with two of his predecessors, namely Mansa Wati and Mansa Khalifa. Perhaps this indicates the instability and dynastic conflicts that are said to have prevailed in the empire at that time. Records are generally silent on the activities or achievements of Mansa Abu Bakr.

Upon the death of Mansa Abu Bakr, another major deviation occurred in the line of succession. A former slave, named Sakura, is said to have captured the throne. Mansa Sakura ruled from 1285 until the end of the century. Although Sakura was apparently from the class of the bondaged, he is said to have risen to a powerful position in the military as well as having become a statesman (Ki-Zerbo, 1978). The exact circumstances of how he managed to gain control of the highest office of the land are mysterious. Ibn Khaldun, on the basis of information from a "most learned, religious, and celebrated" native of Western Sudan whom he had met in Cairo, informs us that Sakura was of servile background. However, upon becoming the ruler, Sakura reversed the malaise that had plagued the empire during the rule of his immediate predecessors. During Sakura's reign, Mali's might was once again asserted in the region and numerous important conquests were successfully undertaken. He subjugated some of the Berber tribes, extended Mali's rule close to the Atlantic Ocean in the region of Senegal, reestablished Mali's control over the gold-producing region of Wangara and Bambuk, and conquered the region of Gao in the east. He followed in the footsteps of Sundiata and Mansa Uli as an empire builder. As a result of the successful conquests undertaken by Sakura, Mali's "authority became mighty and all the peoples of the Sudan stood in awe of them," according to Ibn Khaldun (Levtzion & Hopkins, 1981). With the restoration of order within the empire, increased trade and prosperity followed. However, Sakura's life had an unfortunate end. He died at the hands of brigands who frequently attacked and robbed the trade caravans. They murdered him in the Sahara as he and his entourage were returning from a pilgrimage to Mecca. It is suggested by some scholars that his body was brought back to Mali where he was buried with dignity and respect befitting a monarch.

After the death of the usurper Sakura, the line of succession passed back to the descendants of Sundiata. The throne then went to Mansa Qu, who was the son of Mansa Uli and a grandson of

Sundiata. His reign was a fairly short one of approximately five years. Records do not provide much information on his reign except that he is said to have ruled from 1300-1305. He was in turn succeeded by his son Muhammad Qu, who ruled for another five years or so. It appears that these two rulers held on to an intact empire. Muhammad Qu was the last king before the accession of Mansa Musa. Once again, we find some variations in the literature regarding the year Mansa Musa became the king. Some scholars use 1307 and others use 1312 (See Niane, 1984 and Levtzion, 1963). The accession of Mansa Musa to the throne of Mali is discussed in detail in a later chapter.

Thus, by the time of Mansa Musa's accession, the empire of Mali had been well established. It had been in existence as a major kingdom for seventy-five years since the victory against the Soso at Krina. During these seventy-five years, seven Mansas had succeeded Sundiata. Three of these were Sundiata's sons, one was Sundiata's daughter's son, one was a freed slave who had usurped the throne, and the final two were a son and grandson of Sundiata's eldest son Mansa Uli. This mix of rulers represented four patterns of succession in a relatively short span of time—the patrilineal, the fratrilineal, the matrilineal, and succession through usurpation. The following chart illustrates these patterns:

SUNDIATA

(2)Mansa Uli   (3)Mansa Wati   (4)Khalifa   Daughter

(5) Abu Bakr

(6) Sakura (Ex-slave)

(7) Mansa Qu

(8) Muhammad Qu

All of the above rulers were from the Keita clan of the Malinke. The empire of Mali had become the most dominant political entity in Western Sudan by the end of the thirteenth century. Its predominance or hegemony had expanded to include the ancient empire of Ghana, the major gold fields, the Taghaza salt mines and numerous trading cities that had formed part of the trans-Saharan trade network. In the period following Sundiata, the Malinke territories had been transformed from a network of an alliance of various chiefly states to an imperial system with a center, Kangaba, and dependent states and provinces (Levtzion, 1980). The word Mali, which in the local language merely meant the location where the king resided, came to signify a towering achievement in the West African political history.

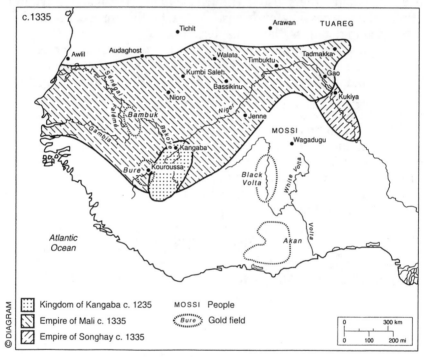

Empire of Mali

One of the issues that remains a matter of contention among historians with respect to several of the ancient African states and civilizations is the issue of the racial identity of the founders of the ruling dynasties of some of these states. For instance, with respect to ancient Ghana, there continues to exist some uncertainties regarding the identity of its original founding dynasty. One school of thought leans towards the non-black origin of ancient Ghanaian rulers, although accepting that it later was ruled by the black kings belonging to the Soninke people of

Western Sudan. This school uses references that are found in the sixteenth and seventeenth century *Tarikhs* that were written by Western Sudanese scholars of Timbuktu and Jenne who attribute a white origin to the founders of ancient Ghana. Perhaps, according to this school, the lighter- skinned Berbers of North and Northwest Africa had established their domination upon the Western Sudanese black population and had made possible the emergence of ancient Ghana. The second school of thought rejects this view of the non-black origin of ancient Ghana by pointing out that all the early Arabic references to ancient Ghana between the eighth and twelfth centuries describe it as a black kingdom by referring to it as the *Bilad as-Sudan*—the land of the black people. Secondly, this school of thought rejects this view of the non-black origin of ancient Ghana on the basis that the light-skinned Berber neighbors of the black Sudanese were basically nomadic peoples and had not yet developed states or empires.

The history of the origin of ancient Mali's ruling dynasty, on the other hand, is not burdened with this sort of question. Mali was and has been viewed as undoubtedly the creation of black people of Western Sudan. Even when some Malian traditions have claimed an outside origin for their kings such as in the case of a tradition that says that the Keita clan (Sundiata's clan) descended from Bilal, the companion of the Prophet Muhammad, it is noteworthy that they are claiming a black origin for Mali's founding dynasty. Bilal was the Abyssinian slave who became converted to Islam in its early days.

What sort of an empire was ancient Mali? What were its political institutions and characteristics? What were its cities like? What were the relations between the kings and the people? What sort of interactions existed between the natives of Mali and outsiders? What was their agricultural economy like? Needless to say, these and many other important questions regarding the nature of this Western African empire come to mind as we attempt to compile and understand its history. For the period prior to the accession of Mansa Musa, we have no choice but to describe the characteristics of ancient Mali in fairly general terms because the ancient sources provide minimal descriptions. We know from its successful conquests and victories that it became militarily the strongest and most powerful state in the region. It had developed a large and a well-armed force. We also know that its economic prosperity depended upon the control of and participation in the trans-Saharan trade network, especially the southern termini. We know that Islam had become a significant influence in the empire though opinions differ as to the extent of this Islamic influence. The ancient written sources focus a bit more on these aspects of the history of Mali. However, for the period after the 1300s, the ancient records are much more helpful. We find in these sources many details that help us understand what type of a society existed in ancient Mali. These sources inform us about education, housing, foods, travel, slavery and slave trade, religion, currencies, clothing, and a few other aspects of the day-to-day lifestyles of the people and the rulers of ancient Mali. These are described in the following chapters. We will first examine in some detail the famous trans-Saharan trade and its importance.

CHAPTER II

THE TRANS-SAHARAN TRADE

Introduction

Africa is the second largest continent in the world. Its size is approximately 11 million square miles. Out of this, nearly 3.5 million square miles are taken up by the Sahara Desert, making it the largest desert in the world. Thus nearly a third of the African land mass, almost the entire northern third, is covered by the vast Sahara. The Sahara extends all across the continent from the Atlantic to the Red Sea covering a distance of about 3,200 miles from the west to the east. In the northeast, the desert reaches the proximity of the shores of the Mediterranean Sea, while in the northwest the Atlas mountains serve as a barrier between the Sahara and the sea. In the south the Sahara extends to below the great bend of the middle Niger, a distance of over one thousand miles. The desert runs through eleven countries on the continent. Immediately along the southern border of the hard-core desert is the region known as the Sahel. This is the area where the desert seems to continue to expand slowly but at an alarming pace. The expanding desert has already caused the displacement of thousands of people and consumed scores of villages and towns. One recent study suggests that the Sahara has expanded from approximately 8.6 million square kilometers in 1980 to approximately 9.3 million square kilometers in 1990 resulting in the growth in the size of the desert by about 6 per cent (Tucker et al., 1991). Traveling through the region one can easily observe this process of desiccation. The Saharan landscape is dotted with isolated semi-fertile oases, several regions of significant mountainous terrain, and a major depression that constitutes the lowest point on the African continent. The mountain ranges include the Tibesti Massif whose highest peak, Emi Koussi, rises to the height of slightly over 11,000 feet. The Tibesti mountains are of volcanic formation. The second important range is the Ahaggar mountains whose highest peak, the Tahat, rises to nearly 9,900 feet. Located in southern Algeria, the Ahaggar range is extremely arid and rocky. In the northwest of Egypt is located the Qattarah Depression, a largely sandy area containing some salt lakes and marshlands. It is approximately 440 feet below sea level. In some parts of the desert the sand dunes are said to be so large that they rise to the height of over 400 feet.

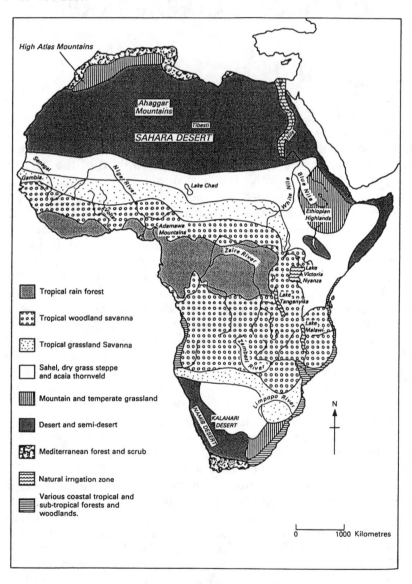

Africa: Vegetation

The desert, of course, is primarily characterized by little or no rainfall at all in large areas for long periods of time. When it does rain, flash floods can be quite common. Occasional snowfall is not unusual at higher elevations. Contrary to general impressions that deserts are always hot, temperatures fluctuate over a wide range from freezing level to as high as 132 degrees. The northern half of the desert is found in the subtropical zone and, therefore, experiences more cooler weather than the southern half which is in the tropical zone. The desert is almost entirely rainless and for the most part devoid of surface water and vegetation except in the oases areas. Wells often have to be dug hundreds of feet before reaching water.

Although the harsh environment of the Sahara has evolved over many thousands of years, the desert has not always been so harsh and dry. Many millennia ago it was lush and supported human life as well as a wide range of plant and animal life. Even as recently as between five to ten thousand years ago, it is believed that the Sahara contained a great quantity of water and was lush with vegetation. About seven thousand years ago, the Sahara is said to have experienced a wet period characterized by innumerable wide and reliable rivers; forests of oak and cypress trees; and savannah-like grasslands teeming with a wide variety of wild game (Davidson, 1972). This wet period is said to have lasted for two to three thousand years.

The major causes of the drying up and desiccation of the Sahara are attributed to both natural as well as human factors. Change in the global weather patterns over the centuries is said to have been the most significant natural cause. Decreasing rainfall and land erosion are some of the other natural causes. Human activities such as overgrazing and deforestation have also played major havoc on the landscape.

Tassili n'Ajjer

The Sahara at one time was very habitable and supported many settlements. Within the past century or so modern archaeologists and explorers have uncovered several sites bearing some very exciting evidence of life in this ancient period. These sites provide fascinating clues to the existence of important cultures in the regions of the Sahara that are so forbidding and desolate today. Perhaps the most important of these sites is the Tassili n'Ajjer, which means plateau of the rivers in the Tuareg language (Lhote, 1963). Located in southeastern Algeria, parts of the Tassili present such a hostile environment that it is hard to believe that a flourishing culture existed there at any time in the past. Heinrich Barth, a nineteenth century European explorer, first reported the existence of the rock art of the Sahara. Yolande Tschundi and Henri Lhote's expeditions in the 1950s exposed to the modern world the richness of Tassili's past (Ritchie, 1979). Most of the evidence of the Tassili's past is depicted in the thousands of rock paintings that have been found there. Modern scholars do not agree on the age of these paintings. Most to accept that the earliest of the Tassili paintings are from the period of 7,000 to 6,000 B.C. Some scholars give these paintings more recent dates. The site has been described as "the world's greatest prehistoric art gallery" (Davidson, 1971). Nearly thirty thousand rock carvings and paintings, some of them of huge dimensions, are estimated to have survived throughout the Sahara.

Peoples from both Europe and Africa are said to have settled in the Sahara in antiquity. The so-called "Europoids" seem to have predominated in the northern regions, whereas Tassili itself is believed to have been settled by black African peoples. In fact, according to Lhote, some of the Tassili paintings have a remarkable resemblance to certain modern-day West Africans. "The horned mask worn (by some figures in the paintings) is striking evidence for the presence of Negroes in the Sahara. Masks of the same type are still worn by Sienuf of the Ivory Coast" (Lhote, 1963). Also, the hairstyles of the women painted on the walls of the Tassili show similarities with the hairstyles many modern West African women.

The Tassili paintings reveal many fascinating details. Perhaps the earliest inhabitants of the Tassili region arrived there about 7,000 B.C. They were a Neolithic culture and survived through hunting and gathering. The paintings dated from this period have been interpreted to suggest an evolutionary pattern in the lifestyle and perhaps in the identity of the ancient Tassilians. The earliest paintings and engravings are associated with the hunting phase of the inhabitants' lifestyle. Abundant wildlife are depicted on these paintings—hippopotami, elephants, giraffes, buffaloes, crocodiles and others. The hunters and gatherers were then followed by the arrival of pastoralists from somewhere in the east. They are said to have resembled some of the modern inhabitants of the Horn of Africa, particularly the Somalis. The pastoralists inaugurated a more settled way of life by establishing villages and began a modicum of sedentary civilization. The first pastoralist settlers are believed to have arrived with goats and sheep, and cattle were introduced later. There are vivid scenes in the paintings that show the pastoralist and the herding phase with the presence of cattle and sheep. Many of these paintings demonstrate a high degree of realism. Scenes of humans show a taste for jewelry. The use of necklaces, pendants and bracelets was apparently quite widespread. Humans are also depicted in positions of copulation, dancing and playing, drawing well water, engaged in combat and performing ceremonies and rituals. Another interesting observation to make is that there are a few paintings that hint at some distant similarities with the ancient Egyptian civilization—particularly, the depiction of humans with animal heads reminiscent of the animal- headed gods and goddesses of the Nile valley. This pastoral period is regarded as the golden age of the Tassili and the most significant civilization of the central Sahara. Thus, Tassili was an important center of human activity in antiquity. The pastoral period is said to have lasted for about two thousand years. Lhote suggests that in that era, the Sahara was the land of abundance. It experienced heavy rainfall and attracted waves of settlers from all directions who engaged in varied activities. In fact, he further suggests, the Sahara was so fertile during that epoch and the settlements were so numerous that the population density in the Sahara was perhaps greater than most of the other regions of the world at that time (Lhote, 1963).

Finally, in the Tassili paintings there are scenes of horses and chariots with armed riders which are taken to suggest invasions from outside. What drove the inhabitants of the Tassili region from their habitat is not quite clear. Combination of the desiccation that was occurring and the arrival of invaders who themselves could not remain there for long due to desiccation are regarded as the major causes for the abandonment of the Tassili region. The invaders, according to some scholars, are said to have originated in Crete, which is quite a distance. Other scholars reject the theory of the Cretan origin. With the progressive harshening of the environment, the population dispersed in different directions. The black African groups by and large are said to have migrated towards the Western Sudan, and the lighter-skinned peoples, principally some of the Berbers, moved up further north and west. But it must be remembered that the lines were not drawn quite so neatly.

The wealth of the rock paintings that have been found at Tassili is not matched by other archaeological finds that could provide more definite answers to the Tassili culture. No tombs or skeletal remains have been found in the vicinity of the painted Tassili rocks. Until such time as additional clues are found, we will continue to have many mysteries about the artists who left such a rich legacy at Tassili. However, the onset of the desert, which dates back to more than two thousand years before the common era, had taken on a life of its own, and the process is an ongoing one. A remarkable illustration of this desiccation is what has happened to Lake Chad which is believed to have shrunk from a size of nearly 116,000 square miles to its present size of approximately 10,000 square miles (Lhote, 1963). However, the desert is believed to contain rich deposits of mineral wealth and a few million people continue to make the Sahara their permanent home.

The Sahara

Despite the fact that there were human settlements in the desert several millennia ago and that there were movements of population groups within the desert region, no descriptions about the desert or the changing conditions in the region have come down to us from any of the earliest inhabitants of the desert. In fact, even the name Sahara came to be applied to this desert only since the coming of the Arabs to the region in the seventh century A.D. Our earliest written accounts about the Sahara and the lands to the south of it come from the ancient Greco-Roman authors. The Carthaginians, who dominated parts of the North African coast for several centuries before the Greeks and the Romans, do not seem to have left any accounts about lands to the south of their zone of occupation. A Carthaginian by the name of Mago is said to have traversed across the desert three times, but no confirmed evidence is available of these crossings (Warmington, 1981). It has also been suggested by some scholars that the Carthaginians were a very secretive people, especially about their trade in the region, and therefore may not have been inclined to reveal to the rest of the world what they knew about their neighbors.

The ancient Greeks and Romans referred to the interior region of North Africa as Inner Libya or Inner Ethiopia (Salama, 1981). The information referring to the region of the Sahara found in the writings of these ancient Greek and Roman writers is rather scant and quite limited. The ancient Greeks were acquainted with parts of the African continent and with some of the African peoples whom they referred to as Ethiopians. They had much more intimate knowledge about Egypt and lands to the south of Egypt along the Nile. Africa to the west of the Nile, except for the Mediterranean coast, was largely unknown. In the accounts of Herodotus, who lived in the fifth century B.C. and had traveled to Egypt, we find references to several groups of people who lived in the region of Libya, along the coast as well as in the interior. One of these interior groups of people he refers to were called the Garamantes who, according to Herodotus, riding in horse-drawn chariots hunted another group, described as Troglodytes (Herodotus, 1992). In these accounts there are brief descriptions about some of the customs of the people, the approximate distances in days between numerous locations, and some of the vegetation. Herodotus made a brief reference to the Sahara Desert by stating that beyond the coastal region of Libya the country was full of wild creatures and beyond that country "there is a tract which is wholly sand, very scant of water, and utterly and entirely a desert" (Herodotus, 1992).

The Romans had a more extensive and a longer period of contact with Africa. Their presence in and knowledge about the continent extended to regions beyond the Nile valley. Actually it was in the western half of the Mediterranean coast of Africa that the Roman involvement with Africa first began. As the Roman Republic grew stronger and more of a factor in the politics and economics of the Mediterranean, it challenged the power and domination of Carthage. Located near the present day city of Tunis, Carthage was founded by Phoenician settlers approximately seven to eight centuries before Christ. Over the years, Carthage developed into a major regional economic and military power that dominated commerce in the Mediterranean and controlled an empire that extended from northwest Africa into parts of Spain. Ancient accounts even mention the possible circumnavigation of the African continent by Phoenician sailors. Carthage practiced a very protectionist trade policy which denied other states access to its lucrative trade and port facilities. As Rome grew in power it rose to challenge the Carthaginian hegemony, and a series of wars, known as the Punic Wars, took place between the two city states in the third century B.C. The renowned Carthaginian leader, Hannibal, led an army of elephants across the Alps during the Second Punic War, but to no avail. The victory went to the Romans. These wars continued on and off until the final destruction of Carthage by Rome and its allies in 146 B.C. Eventually, the Roman rule expanded across North Africa, including the conquest of Egypt in 30 B.C. Thus, at the height of Roman power, its control extended all along the North African coast from Morocco to Egypt. In Egypt it extended furthest into the interior where it came into contact with the ancient state of Meroe. In other parts of North Africa its control was confined largely to areas close to the coast. Southward expansion was checked by the Sahara Desert.

However, the Romans were forced to deal with the desert and to penetrate southward into the desert in order to crush the local opposition to the Roman rule. Military necessity required the Romans to face the challenges of the Sahara. They had built a series of defense posts fifty to a hundred kilometers into the interior from the Mediterranean coast. But these were not enough to keep the North African tribes at bay. Therefore, several punitive and invasive expeditions are recorded to have been undertaken by the Roman army. It is suggested that one of these military expeditions, led by Julius Maternus, may have even crossed the desert all the way up to Lake Chad (Snowden, 1970). The writings of Pliny the Elder and Claudius Ptolemy provide some information about northern Africa but not much about the Sahara.

One very important development that occurred during the Roman domination of northern Africa was the introduction of the camel into the western part of north Africa. The camel was to revolutionize the history of the Sahara as well as the lands to the north and the south of it. The camel is said to have been first introduced into Africa in Egypt during the Persian conquest in the sixth century B.C. It would take eight to nine hundred more years before it spread to western parts of the Sahara. The reasons for such long delay are not very clear. None of the earliest records, written or painted on rocks, show the presence of the camel in northern Africa or in the Sahara in the earliest period. On the contrary, the elephant, an animal least likely to be associated with northern Africa, was more extensively used such as in the case of the Carthaginian leader Hannibal's army during the Second Punic War against Rome. The Romans introduced the camel into parts of North Africa outside of Egypt sometime during the first three centuries of the Christian era. However, the Roman use of the camel was more for military rather than commercial reasons.

Consequently, our earliest detailed and extensive descriptive accounts about the Sahara had to await the coming of the Arabs. After the Arabs established their control and domination over northern Africa during the seventh century A.D., their influence and presence gradually spread across the Sahara. The Berbers were and are up to the present time the most numerous inhabitants of the western parts of the Sahara. After they became converted to Islam and adopted the Arabic language, they contributed much by way of leaving important written accounts about the Sahara, its inhabitants, its economy, conflicts and other topics. One of the most valuable of these accounts about the Sahara and the peoples and states that were linked with it is the work of the fourteenth century Berber traveler Ibn Battuta. His is the first detailed description of the crossing of this vast desert from Morocco to the countries along the Niger River region. His eyewitness testimony has contributed much to our understanding of the trans-Saharan trade and life in ancient Mali. His account will be extensively used and summarized in the succeeding chapters of this book. Prior to Ibn Battuta, Ibn Hawkal had visited parts of the Western Sudan during the tenth century and recorded his impressions and Al-Bakri wrote about the region in the eleventh century.

Later on, other travelers, most notably Leo Africanus in the sixteenth century, also wrote detailed accounts about the trans-Saharan geography, trade and cultures. The first European explorers and travelers to cross the Sahara and report on the Western Sudanese societies did so in the nineteenth century. In 1819, Captain George Lyon trekked about 1,400 miles from Tripoli south through the desert. He had a most miserable experience as he suffered intensely due to heat, lack of water, and a variety of illnesses. In 1822, the team of Dixon Denham, Hugh Clapperton and Walter Oudney traveled from Tripoli to Lake Chad. In 1826, Major Gordon Laing's attempt to cross the desert ended with his murder near Timbuktu. The Frenchman Rene Caillie, posing as an Arab, successfully reached Timbuktu in 1828 and went on to cross the desert from Timbuktu to Fez in Morocco. Probably the most noteworthy of the European explorers was Heinrich Barth, a German, who traveled in the region in the 1850s. He made detailed observations about the geology, flora and fauna, and some cultural aspects of the peoples (Swift, 1995). Accounts of all these writers help us put together to some extent the story of ancient Mali and the life and times of Mansa Musa.

Trade Across the Desert

One important fact about ancient Mali is that its rise to power and claim to fame was to a great degree linked to the trans-Saharan trade. The last few pages briefly describing some historical information about this desert have set the stage for an in-depth survey of the trans-Saharan trade. In the following few pages, the nature of the trans-Saharan trade, its commodity composition, its routes, and its impact are explored. Using a wide range of sources from ancient, medieval, and modern historians and writers, a general picture about the trade across the desert and the role that ancient Mali played in it is presented here.

As mentioned earlier, the Sahara Desert, despite its massive size and harshness, has not prevented human beings from living in it or traveling and trading through it. The desert has not been an insurmountable barrier. Exactly for how long the long-distance trans-Saharan trade has been going on is unclear. Its importance to ancient Carthage and the Roman Empire seems to have been quite minimal according to some scholars. Modern scholars differ on the matter of establishing the antiquity of the trans-Saharan trade. For instance, Hopkins (1973) suggests that the

> trans-Saharan trade between West and North Africa began as early as 1,000 B.C. when desert crossing was made by oxen and by chariots or carts drawn by horses. The trade was developed by the Carthaginians from about the fifth century B.C. and was given further impetus by the Romans three centuries later.

A more recent analysis of the trans-Saharan trade suggests that the regular connections between the Mediterranean region and the Western Sudanese region did not develop until the seventh century A.D., and this happened partly due to the rapid spread of the use of the camel. According to this source, the camel "was the only animal that could have made possible the long rides of between one and two thousand kilometers between the two verges of the Sahara. Neither chariots, horse, donkeys nor the slow-moving draught oxen attested by rock art met the needs of difficult, heavy, long-distance trade" (Hrbek, 1992). Andah suggests that there is evidence of Roman trade in ivory and slaves with the Sudan (1984).

Some of the ancient Greek and Roman sources make mention of trade in carbuncles, precious stones, between the coast of Libya and the interior peoples known as Garamantes, Troglodytes and Nasamones (Salama, 1981). Herodotus, in the fifth century B.C., described the trade between the Carthaginians and a country beyond the "Pillars of Heracles" (Straits of Gibraltar) which is thought to have been along the western coast of Africa.

Herodotus' description is rather brief, but he does mention two characteristics of this trade that were to become two of the identifying attributes of the trans-Saharan trade for many years later. He mentioned the inclusion of gold as an important commodity in this trade and, secondly, he described the way the trade was conducted. Later, in the writings of several Arab authors, similar descriptions were recorded.

The way this trade was conducted, as described by Herodotus, has been referred to as "dumb barter" or "silent trade." When the Carthaginians came to the shores of the country beyond the "Pillars of Heracles," they unloaded their merchandise, displayed it on the beach, went back to their boat and sent out smoke signals to the natives. Upon seeing the signals, the natives came and laid down whatever amount of gold they thought the merchandise left by the first group was worth and then they withdrew. The Carthaginians would then return, and if they were satisfied by the amount of gold left by the natives, they took it, indicating that a deal was done. But if they were not satisfied with the amount of gold left, they did not touch the gold and retreated once again and waited for the native to add more gold. This process would go on until a deal was made. Neither party took the other trader's merchandise until it was felt that the deal was a fair exchange (Herodotus, 1992).

Thus, while uncertainties remain as to the origin, the extent and the composition of the trade across the Sahara in the period before two thousand years ago, it is generally agreed that trade within narrower regions in northern and western Africa did take place. Thus extensive local trade networks were in place that expanded into or rapidly linked up with the trans-Saharan trade under the right conditions and opportunities. The development of the technology of iron by the fourth century B.C. is said to have played an important role in the growth of the local trade networks. Iron tools increased agricultural production resulting in food surpluses in certain regions which were channeled into local trade networks.

In the history of world civilizations trade has served as a major agent and a catalyst for the rise or the decline of societies. On the positive side, trade results in the introduction of new commodities; development of newer relationships between different peoples; introduction of new ideas; creation of wealth; growth of cities; transmission of new cultures and ways of life; and improvement in the quality and standards of living. On the negative side, trade could result in rivalries between peoples;

exploitation; development of classes based on wealth; wars for the control of resources; and loss of traditional cultures and values. The trans-Saharan trade was no exception. It impacted the peoples on both sides of the Sahara in a number of positive and negative ways.

As the use of the camel across the northern half of Africa spread during the latter part of the Roman period, it ultimately had a great impact on the ability of people to move across the desert. The introduction of the camel has been acknowledged by the scholars as an occurrence of the greatest importance. Bovill describes it as "an event of such far-reaching consequences that it marked the dawn of a new era for the northern half of the continent" (1970). Camels "proved providential for all the nomads, who were handicapped by the drawbacks of the horse at a time when the climate was becoming alarmingly drier" (Salama, 1981). According to Gautier, "the appearance of this animal proved to be the turning point in the history of the (Sahara) desert itself, the great event which caused a radical transformation in its destiny. Historically we may say there are two Saharas: the precameline Sahara, and the modern or cameline Sahara" (1970). The camel turned out to be an ideal animal for the desert. Its ability to cover more distance in the sand with relative ease, to carry more weight, and to travel for longer periods without water were all the qualities that suited the desert environment. And according to some accounts, in times of extreme hardship in the desert due to lack of water, a camel could be sacrificed for the benefit of man for the water stored in its body. Only the introduction of the modern motor car would surpass the importance of the camel for crossing the desert overland.

The Berbers, who had remained as a dominant population, used it to enhance their mobility and power in the desert. Thus the Berbers and Berber-speaking groups became much more involved in the conduct of the trans-Saharan trade. One of the major handicaps we have in discussing or assessing the importance of the trans-Saharan trade during different time periods is the fact that there are no statistics available about the trade. Therefore, we can only talk about it in a general sense that either shows an increased or expanded trade during certain periods or a declining trade during other periods. The camel is regarded as the factor that enabled the development of a continuous link between the Western Sudan and the Mediterranean Africa. So, with the entry of the camel, the trade is said to have increased across the Sahara during the latter part of the Roman era. Several important routes evolved that linked the

Western Sudanese, Saharan and North African trading centers. The most direct route in the east is said to have been the one which linked Tripoli with the oases of Murzuk and Bilma and then to the region of Lake Chad (Porch, 1984). Other routes linked Morocco with central Niger and Upper Senegal.

Even though the camel made the crossing of the desert relatively easy, it must be emphasized that it was always a challenging and a daunting task to make the journey. Traversing the Sahara could be a "murderous business" for it involved vast distances, torturous weather, food and water scarcity, and treacherous sandstorms. Each journey meant a battle for survival. Ibn Hawkal mentioned in the 900s that more than one caravan had perished in the desert due to severe sandstorms (Levtzion & Hopkins, 1981). Those who succeeded in doing it and who left written accounts of their journeys, such as Ibn Battuta, Rene Caillie and others, have given us vivid and horrifying details of their ordeals. I had one brief experience in the Sahara on the way to Timbuktu and it proved to be the most frightening experience of my life. Our group got lost in the desert for about half a day and with gasoline, food and water running out, the level of our fright reached the maximum.

Herodotus and a few other Greco-Roman writers have given us information about this early trade between the Mediterranean Africa and the interior Africa. Gold, precious stones, animals and animal products, agricultural products, metal objects, pottery, textiles and glassware were among the more important items. Some trade in African slaves is also said to have taken place.

Impact of the Arab Conquest of North Africa

The trans-Saharan trade experienced a phenomenal growth in its value and volume after the conquest of North Africa by the Arabs in the seventh century. Like the introduction of the camel earlier, the Arab invasion and domination of North Africa served as a major transforming factor in the history of North as well as West Africa. There is no disagreement among scholars about the significance of this development upon the trans-Saharan trade. According to Hopkins, "The rise of the Arab power from the seventh century onwards, though at first a destabilizing influence on North African politics, eventually contributed substantially to the growth of trans-Sahara commerce" (1973). The religious impact of this invasion will be explored in the next chapter. In the next few pages a review of the political and economic consequences of the Arab expansion are in order.

The expansion and outflow of the Arabs and their civilization beyond the confines of the Arabian peninsula coincided with the establishment of Islam as the new creed of Arabia. Prophet Muhammad, who lived during the period 570 to 632, shaped the religion of Islam on the basis of revelations that came to him in Mecca and Medina from Allah starting from A.D. 610. By the time of Prophet Muhammad's death, the religion and the hegemony of Islam had been extended to about a third of the western regions of the Arabian peninsula. Within the next decade the Prophet's successors expanded their state and through conquests built in a very short span of time one of the largest empires the world has seen. They very rapidly conquered parts of what are today the countries of Syria, Israel, Palestine, Iraq and Iran. In the span of a single decade "a host of highly organized, sophisticated, and settled societies found themselves conquered by migratory Arab tribesmen" (Garrity & Gay, 1972). Within a century, the Arab armies conquered all of the Mediterranean region of North Africa and Spain to the west and parts of the former Byzantine Empire and Sassanian Empire to the east. In Europe the Arab/Islamic expansion was halted in France in A.D. 732 at the Battle of Tours.

The Arab conquest of North Africa started with the conquest of Egypt in A.D. 639 under the leadership of Amr ibn al-As with a force of about 3,500 soldiers. Egypt and other parts of North Africa were under Byzantine control at the time. While the establishment of the Arab rule in Egypt came about rather rapidly, it took longer to spread over the rest of North Africa. Their advance across the continent beyond Libya encountered significant resistance from the Berber communities. Under the leadership, first of Kosaila and later of a woman leader known as Kahina, the Berbers slowed the Arab advance. It was not until almost the end of the seventh century that the Berber resistance was overcome. However, along the way some Berbers had been converted to Islam and had joined the Arab army. After the subjugation of the Berbers, the Islamic army, consisting of Arabs, Berbers and black Africans, crossed the Straits of Gibraltar and conquered Spain in 711. Berbers, after the conversions to Islam, were to play a vital role in carrying the message of Islam to Western Sudan. Furthermore, the Berbers were also to experience other dynamics associated with the overall history of Islam—i.e. the growth of fundamentalist movements; the rise of numerous dynasties and conflicts among them; and the establishment of new cities with flourishing artistic and intellectual culture.

What were the reasons and factors that contributed to the swift rise and success of the Arab expansion? Scholars point to several major factors. Desire to spread the new religion certainly played a part. The existing major empires, Byzantine and Sassanian, had been warring with each other for years and therefore they had weakened considerably. Many of the subjects of these two empires were under various forms of persecution and oppression and they welcomed the Arabs as liberators. Motives of greed also played a part. According to Mansfield, "There were two main impulses behind its expansion: the need to find an outlet for the martial energies of the beduin warriors and the search for booty and supplies to sustain the impoverished community" (1980).

Thus, within a century, the Bedouin Arabs, who until the life of Prophet Muhammad had remained on the sidelines of the major developments in the history of the Middle East from the time of ancient Mesopotamia to the Byzantine period, made a pronounced appearance on the stage of world history. The Arabic language, religion and culture came to dominate a good portion of the world from the Straits of Gibraltar to the gates of China and India. At the same time Islam became a multiethnic, multinational and multiracial civilization.

Gradually over the next several centuries after the conquest of North Africa, the Arab and Islamic influence made its way across the Sahara to the Western Sudan. In the first instance, as far as Western Sudan is concerned, the Arabic influence was more significant in the realm of economic relations, particularly in the trans-Saharan trade. After the wars of conquests had subsided, regional economies flourished. Conversions were to take place as well, but they came somewhat later.

As the Arabic and Islamic influence spread to North and West Africa, the first written references about the trade, along with information about some other aspects of these countries, began to be recorded. Over the next several centuries the trade multiplied several times. New market cities were established and some smaller ones grew to more importance. The trade brought fame to the ancient empire of Ghana. In order to boost the trade, an Arab governor of a North African province even undertook to establish wells along certain routes. The pattern of the trans-Saharan trade which, in general, was to remain fairly constant for many centuries, became well established in these early centuries of Islamic hegemony. In many ways it followed the pattern that some scholars said existed during the latter part of the Roman period.

The trade followed about half a dozen routes that linked Western Sahara with North Africa. The earliest written references to specific routes were recorded by Al-Yaqubi in the 800s (Levtzion and Hopkins, 1981). Based upon his own visit to North Africa, he made mention of two trade routes—one from Zawila in southern Sahara and the other from Sijilmasa in northern Sahara. Of the route from Sijilmasa, Al-Yaqubi wrote as follows:

> He who travels from Sijilmasa towards the south, making for the land of the Sudan (which is inhabited by different tribes of the Sudan) goes in a desert of 50 stages. Then he will be met in the desert by a people called Anbiya, of the Sanhaja, who have no permanent dwellings. It is their custom to veil their faces with their turban. They do not wear (sewn) clothes, but wrap themselves in lengths of cloth. They subsist on camels, for they have no crops, wheat or otherwise. Then the traveler will reach a town called Ghust which is in an inhabited valley with dwellings. It is the residence of their king, who has no religion or law. He raids the land of the Sudan, who have many kingdoms. (Levtzion & Hopkins, 1981)

Incidentally, Al-Yaqubi also makes one of the earliest references to Malal (regarded by scholars as to mean Mali). Al-Yaqubi referred to ancient Ghana as the country of many gold mines.

Ibn Hawkal, who traveled to Northwest Africa in the 900s and recorded his accounts of some of the cities involved in the trans-Saharan trade, made references to three important routes. One, along the east-west direction, connected Kayrawan in Tunisia with Sijilmasa in Morocco; the second route was down south to ancient Ghana and Mali; and the third one connected Western Sudan with Libya in the northeast (Hrbek, 1992). There were routes that went from ancient Mali via Timbuktu to Fez (Morocco) and Ifriqiya (Tunisia), and from Timbuktu and Gao to Tripoli and Cairo and to Lake Chad. A close and detailed scrutiny of the early Arabic authors gives us information about changes in the importance of certain routes over the others over time or about the demise of some routes and development of new ones. Thus, over

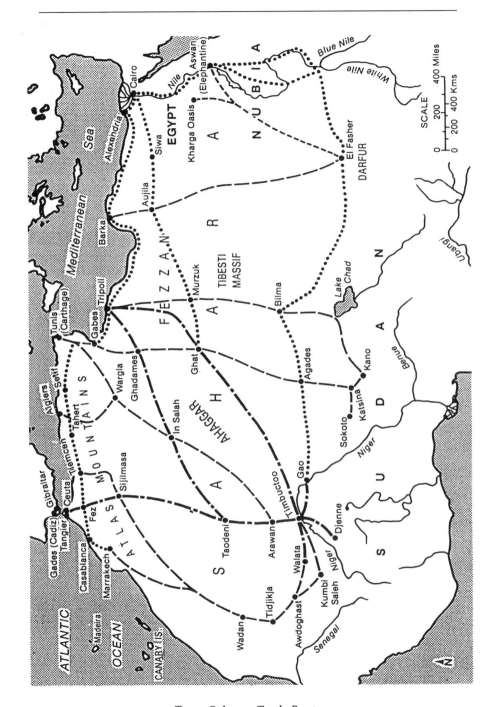

Trans-Saharan Trade Routes

the centuries a vast network of trade linking many cities, oases, villages, and centers of production evolved. Ironically, as one scholar has pointed out, more inter-continental communications took place across the Sahara over the centuries between Western Sudan and North Africa than in the regions that were blessed with friendlier environments.

Some general observations about the characteristics and the nature of the trans-Saharan trade are now in order. The trade was basically a barter-type trade which meant that merchants traded commodities for commodities. Certain commodities seemed to have been used more commonly and uniformly and, therefore, they have been equated by some modern analysts to currencies. Gold coins or gold dust, cowry shells, pieces of cotton cloth and metal ingots are regarded as some of the local currencies in West Africa (Hopkins, 1973). Secondly, the trade was like a relay race where numerous groups and peoples were involved in the middle. So, by the time the goods from the north reached the southernmost termini, they would have been handled by a variety of peoples and vice versa. The Tuaregs, a major group of Berbers who live in the western and the central Sahara, with their mastery of the desert and the camel, were the crucial link in the transportation network. Thus, the prosperity of many peoples was linked with the trade. Sometimes the trade was carried out by the method of "dumb barter" first described by Herodotus in the fifth century B.C. Several Arabic sources also make reference to this practice. This is how Al-Yaquti described it in the early 1200s:

> When they (the merchants from the north) arrive there, they beat great drums which they have brought with them, and which may be heard from the horizon where these people of the Sudan live. It is said that they dwell in underground hiding places and burrows, and that they are naked, like animals, covering (of the body) being unknown to them.... When the merchants know that those people have heard the drum, they produce whatever they have brought of the aforementioned wares and each merchant lays down his own, each kind apart. Then the Sudan come with the gold, put a certain amount of gold alongside each kind and withdraw. Then the merchants come after them and each one takes the gold which he finds beside his merchandise. They

leave the merchandise and depart after having beaten their drums. (Levtzion & Hopkins, 1981)

In Herodotus' description of the "dumb barter" between the Carthaginians and the traders along the coast of northwest Africa, the signal given was the smoke. However, some modern scholars have cast serious doubts on the existence of such practices and have de-emphasized the importance of such reports and accounts.

In many of the trade termini in the Sahel region of the Western Sudan there were communities and settlements of merchants, mostly Muslim Arabs and Berbers from the north who are said to have frequently lived in separate sections of the towns. Al-Bakri in the eleventh century mentioned the existence of a separate Muslim town in ancient Ghana. Ibn Battuta's account also confirmed this division, for he himself often stayed in Muslim sections of some of the towns in Mali.

Finally, the process of the rise and fall of states was a function to some degree of the control of the trans-Saharan trade and trade routes.

The Merchandise of the Trade

The early written records and archaeological evidence provide us with important information about the commodities and merchandise that were involved in this trade. In general this merchandise consisted of food items, manufactured glass, metal objects, textiles, animal products and others. Trade in livestock was also prevalent. But the most important trade items, according to most historical accounts, were salt, gold and slaves. According to Bovill, "Slaves and gold, and gold and slaves, provided the life-blood of the trade of the Maghrib (Northwest Africa) with the Sudan" (1970). Salt was such an important commodity in Western Sudan that there are accounts that inform us that at certain times salt was exchanged for gold for an equal weight. The matter of the slave trade is discussed more fully in a later chapter. Thus, of all the exports from the Western Sudan, gold was among the most valued in the world beyond the Sahara. This is one commodity from the Western Sudan about which all the early Arabic sources make mention.

It was the demand for the West African gold in the Islamic world that is regarded by some modern historians as the engine that propelled the development of the vast network of the trans-Saharan trade. According to more recent research and analysis of the trans-Saharan trade by prominent scholars, important developments occurred in the Islamic world that greatly stimulated the demand for gold which in turn impacted trade across the Sahara. Devisse (1992) concludes that in the period between the seventh and tenth centuries, several Muslim dynasties that ruled in Egypt, Morocco and Spain began the practice of minting gold coins. Most notably, the use of the gold coin by the Fatimid dynasty in Egypt, the Umayyad dynasty in Spain, and the Almoravid dynasty in Morocco and Spain, contributed immensely to the expansion of the demand for the Western Sudanese gold. The Almoravids, who are generally discussed in most books on the history of West Africa in the context of the growth and expansion of their fundamentalist movement and its conquest of ancient Ghana, are regarded by J. Devisse as being responsible for a major expansion in the trans-Saharan gold trade. The Almoravids alone are said to have established twenty-one mints in Morocco and Spain (Devisse, 1992). Moreover, the Western Sudanese gold was regarded as very high-quality material.

Thus, Western Sudan was often referred to as the El Dorado of the old world. Some of the Arab writers, though, had some wild ideas about the West African gold. One author wrote that in ancient Ghana gold grew in the sand like carrots and that people just plucked it out during sunrise (Levtzion & Hopkins, 1981). This impression was first recorded in the early 900s and was subsequently believed and recorded by several other writers in later years. Later on, as the European city states outside of Spain began to mint their own gold coins, they too turned to West Africa for their supplies of gold.

In the history of West Africa there are three major areas that are regarded to have been the most important gold-producing regions. Two of them, Bambuk and Bure, were within Western Sudan and were territories that were conquered and controlled by the ancient empires of Ghana, Mali and Songhay; the third area, the Akan, was located further south in the forest region. While the political and military power of ancient Ghana and Mali did not reach quite this far south, the Akan gold did find its way to the north and across the Sahara. One important point about these gold-rich areas frequently mentioned in the sources is that their exact locations were secret, and foreign traders—Africans or Arabs and Berbers—were generally barred from getting too close to them by the peoples who controlled the rich deposits. The inhabitants of the gold-producing areas seemed to be not only quite secretive about the exact locations of the minerals, but they are also said to have been sensitive to any interference or direct control from the kings in whose empires they happened to be located. If the kings tried to control their gold deposits directly or tried to impose alien culture upon them, it is said that they would stop the production or reduce it considerably.

For the people to the south of the Sahara Desert, salt was a most vital import. Sources make mention of Awlil in the region of Senegal as the earliest and most important source of salt. Later on also Taghaza and other salt mines located in the Sahara Desert became very important sources.

By the time the empire of Mali emerged in the 1230s, and as it evolved during the thirteenth century from the time of Sundiata to the eve of the Mansa Musa era in the early fourteenth century, the trans-Saharan trade had developed to become a major feature of Western Sudan. It provided the link with the outside world and the major source of wealth for the rulers. It provided the economic rationale for the imperial systems.

Early Eyewitness Accounts

Ibn Battuta provides us with an eyewitness account of the traffic across the Sahara and the life in the empire of Mali in the fourteenth century. Ibn Battuta embarked on his journey across the Sahara in 1352. This was his last traveling adventure. Inspired initially by religious devotion, he left his home in Morocco in 1324 to perform the Islamic Pilgrimage to Mecca. Along the way, he developed other interests and did not go to Mecca until after a side trip to Syria. After performing the *hajj* (pilgrimage to Mecca), he continued on with his travels, and during the next thirty years or so he visited many lands in the Islamic world and parts of China and Russia as well. In Africa, he had traveled through North Africa, his home region, and the East African city states of the Swahili prior to the trans-Saharan journey. In 1352, after taking the leave of his sovereign, the Sultan of Morocco, Ibn Battuta departed from Fez for the city of Sijilmasa where he joined a trans-Saharan caravan.

Sijilmasa, a city founded in the eighth century, had become a most important northern terminus in the trans-Saharan trade network. Based upon the prosperity resulting from this trade, the city had become a fairly cosmopolitan center with people having come from as far as Iraq to settle there. Ibn Battuta found the city quite agreeable and lodged there with a man whose brother he

43

claimed to have met in a city in China. He praised the dates of Sijilmasa to be even better than those of Basra in Iraq, and one variety of Sijilmasa dates in particular he judged to be the best in the world. This city was also greatly praised by another prominent writer, Ibn Hawkal, nearly three hundred years earlier. Ibn Hawkal praised its healthy climate and the good manners, morals, charity and scholarly interests of its inhabitants. He described the city as having a busy commercial life (Levtzion & Hopkins, 1981). Sijilmasa was also among the earliest cities in northwest Africa where a mint for gold coinage was established. After making his preparations, such as buying camels and food supplies for four months, Ibn Battuta set out for the crossing of the Sahara in the company of a caravan of merchants in February 1352. He did not comment on the actual size or makeup of the caravan or the types of merchandise they carried.

After traveling for twenty-five days, the caravan arrived at Taghaza. The earlier Arabic sources do not mention Taghaza but by Ibn Battuta's time it had become a major salt-producing area. (The earlier sources mention Awlil, the region of the Senegal, as the major salt-producing area.) Ibn Battuta found Taghaza to be treeless and a very unappealing place with poor quality of water and infested with flies. But there was a lot of salt mining going on there. He remarked that even the houses and mosques were built of blocks of salt. The inhabitants of Taghaza, according to Ibn Battuta, were all slave laborers who worked in the salt mines for their masters, the Massufa, a Berber tribe. The workers lived on dates, camel meat and Sudanese millet. The Sudanese traders from the south came here to obtain salt. By the time this salt made its way to the lands further south, it yielded a price four or five times the original price. The salt, according to Ibn Battuta, was used not only for consumption but also as a medium of exchange. The business conducted at Taghaza was fairly substantial. After a stay of ten uncomfortable days, the caravan stocked up on water supplies and set out for the next destination. Ibn Battuta observed that travelers wore necklaces containing mercury to protect against lice. Along this segment he realized the risk and danger of being separated from the caravan and he became cautious of venturing out on his own. He also described that when the caravan was about four days from the next major town, Walata, a messenger would be sent to the town to alert townspeople about the approach of the caravan in order to arrange for lodging. Sometimes the messengers would die along the way and in that case the arrival of the caravan would be unexpected and a surprise. However, in this particular case, the messenger had made it and a party of the townspeople of Walata had come out to greet the caravan. After a journey of two months from Sijilmasa, the caravan reached Walata.

Walata had become an important terminus after the conquest of Kumbi in ancient Ghana by Sumanguru in the 1220s. The merchants abandoned Kumbi and settled in the safety and tranquillity of Walata. Ibn Battuta described this town as the northernmost area under the control of the Sudanese. It was made a part of the empire of Mali after its conquest by one of Sundiata's successors in the 1200s. It was administered by an official (*farba*) representing the Mansa. The official at the time, Farba Husayn, speaking through an interpreter, greeted the caravan. Ibn Battuta saw this manner of speaking through an interpreter as a sign of contempt and an insult by the Sudanese official towards the white Berbers. Momentarily, he regretted ever having come to this country of the Sudan. Ibn Battuta became even more offended when another official of the town invited the visitors and served a simple local meal prepared from millet, milk and honey served in a calabash bowl. He thought that not much good could be expected from his Sudanese hosts and he seriously contemplated returning to Morocco. He decided not to, however, and things did get better for him during the rest of his stay in Walata. The town, according to Ibn Battuta, was inhabited mostly by Massufa Berbers. The climate was hot and there were few date-palms and plenty of mutton. People wore fine clothes made from imported Egyptian fabric. The women, he remarked, were beautiful and well respected. He also commented that the people practiced the matrilineal pattern of descent, which he regarded as a very unusual custom, especially among Muslims. (It will be recalled that Al-Bakri mentioned the existence of the matrilineal practice among the people of ancient Ghana in the eleventh century.) Another interesting bit of detail about Walata has come to us from the account of Al-Khatib, a contemporary of Ibn Battuta. Al-Khatib was a resident of Granada, Spain. He described a trading enterprise developed and controlled by one family in particular, with business branches in Sijilmasa, Walata and a couple of other cities. They maintained a system of communications whereby they sent information to each other regarding the level of supply and demand of commodities. In this way, they managed to become a very prosperous family. When Walata was conquered by the Mansa of Mali, the king is said to have encouraged and allowed this family to trade in all his lands, and he developed good relations with the merchant's family (Levtzion & Hopkins, 1981).

After a stay of about fifty days, Ibn Battuta departed from Walata for the next phase of his journey to the capital of Mali. He described the changing landscape. He passed through a region with many and large-sized trees. In this region, a traveler did not need to carry food supplies. With some barter goods like salt and glassware, one could obtain a variety of food items in the villages. After ten days' travel from Walata, he arrived at a large village called Zaghari where he found among the population a community of white Berber merchants. Shortly thereafter, he reached the Niger River. The ancient records, both Arabic as well as maps that came out of Europe, showed and referred to both Niger and the Senegal rivers as being extensions of the Nile. There was the belief that the Nile, after it reached beyond the borders of Egypt, continued westwards into Western Sudan. This confusion would persist until the nineteenth century. He even observed a crocodile the size of a small boat. After a bit more wandering about in the country near the river, he came to the capital of the empire of Mali, believed to be the town of Niani.

In the capital of Mali there was a section of the town where the white Berbers resided. There one of them had arranged for a house for Ibn Battuta. In this town, the Moroccan visitor was pleased with the hospitality and gifts that he received from both the Berber residents and Malian officials. A few days after his arrival, he became very sick, apparently from food poisoning. He survived but remained in ill health for the following two months. Ibn Battuta's description of his meeting with and reception by the king of Mali at the time is taken up in a later chapter. Suffice it to state here that he considered the reigning king as a miserly ruler and not the sort who would bestow rich gifts upon visitors. While in Mali, Ibn Battuta was very sensitive about the quantity and quality of gifts given as a measure of the hospitality accorded him.

After a stay of about eight months in the capital of Mali from June 1352 to February 1353, he departed towards the north. Traveling by camel because horses were quite expensive, he continued his trek along and across the Niger River. He commented upon the sighting of hippopotami in the river and the practice of the local people of catching and eating them. He recorded stories and reports about the existence of a cannibalistic group of people in the country. Ibn Battuta also visited the famed city of Timbuktu, still many decades away from its 'golden age.' From there he continued his journey by sailing on the Niger towards the city of Gao. Along the way his party traded for food with the local villagers by exchanging salt, spices, and glass beads.

Before he reached Gao he had the occasion to experience another instance of the hospitality of a Malian official in a town whose name he could not recall. Ibn Battuta was most pleased with his reception by this official, Farba Sulayman, and considered him as the most generous and upright Malian that he had met.

Ibn Battuta's next stop was Gao, the country of the Songhay people. Gao had been conquered earlier by the armies of Mali. Ibn Battuta described Gao as large and one of the nicest towns in the country of the black people which also was well supplied with stocks of rice, milk, fish and the best cucumber variety in the world. He described the use of cowry shells as a currency. After a month's stay there he departed for the next leg of his journey which was now homeward bound. He and his caravan passed through the country of the Bardama Berbers through which, he recorded, no caravan may pass without protection. He reached the copper-producing region of Taggada whose inhabitants were very much involved in the trans-Saharan trade, especially with Egypt. From Taggada he took a side trip to visit the Sultan of that region who received him well and showed him much hospitality. Upon his return to Taggada after this side trip of six days he received a message from his sovereign, the Sultan of Morocco, instructing him to return to his homeland. Thus, he made his preparations to cross the Sahara northwards. He bought his camels and food provisions for seventy days and in September 1353 joined a large caravan for the return journey. Regarding the return journey, he recorded the harsh conditions of the desert, accounts of passage through Berber countries, and a reference to an incident when the caravan was held hostage for ransom by a Berber group. After about three months, the caravan arrived in Sijilmasa. During the rest of his journey to Fez, he encountered very cold and snowy weather. And thus ended one of the most momentous journeys ever by an individual. Ibn Juzzay, the Moroccan scribe who recorded ibn Battuta's narrative, in a postscript described him as the "traveler of the age." Its significance for African history has been time and again recognized by modern scholars.

Although Ibn Battuta did not mention in his accounts the size of the caravans which he accompanied during his crossings of the Sahara or encountering any other caravans along the routes, there is a reference in the writing of Ibn Khaldun that in 1353, the same year that Ibn Battuta was traveling through Mali, he was told about one caravan that was involved in the trans-Saharan trade between Mali and Egypt. Its size was twelve thousand camels (Levtzion, 1980). An early nineteenth century account by an

Englishman who had resided in Morocco for several years reports that in 1805 a caravan consisting of eighteen hundred camels traveling from Timbuktu to Tafilelt perished due to lack of water (Jackson, 1968).

The trans-Saharan trade, while it brought prosperity and fame to ancient Mali and other states through whose territories it was conducted, also was one important factor that contributed to rivalries and conflicts among the states of Western Sudan and Northwest Africa for the control of the trade, especially gold. In the 1590s, the Sultan of Morocco, lured by the desire to control the wealth of the Western Sudan, sent an army across the Sahara in order to establish Moroccan supremacy over the region that once formed part of ancient Mali. In the nineteenth century, numerous European explorers and traders were also inspired by the stories of gold and wealth that was traded in the Western Sudan to venture inland into the interior of West Africa. Thus, the trans-Saharan trade had continued to be significant well into the nineteenth century. The pattern of trade was generally unchanged, although the commodity composition of the trade certainly varied from time to time.

After Ibn Battuta's account about the Western Sudan in the fourteenth century and his observations about the trans-Saharan trade and the crossing of the Sahara desert, our next most important description of the Western Sudan by a person who actually traveled there comes to us from the writings of Leo Africanus in the 1500s. Leo Africanus visited the region after ancient Mali had lost most of its northern territories to the empire of Songhay. He nonetheless sheds important light on the evolution of the Western Sudan including the areas which once were under the rule of the Mansas of Mali and where the rulers and traders of ancient Mali had lain the groundwork for future growth and development. The famed city of Timbuktu was one such place and it is discussed in more detail below. Leo Africanus visited some of the same places that Ibn Battuta had visited about a hundred and fifty years earlier, so this gives some basis to compare the experiences and observations of these two very prominent individuals.

Leo Africanus was one of the most interesting individuals of the sixteenth century. Originally of Muslim background, he was born in Spain in the 1490s, shortly after the victory of King Ferdinand and Queen Isabela against the Muslim-dominated state of Granada in 1492. Granada was among the last regions of Spain to be reconquered by the Christian rulers. Spain, which had been conquered by the Islamic army in the early 700s, became one of the few countries which successfully reversed the Islamic conquest and domination, even though it took several centuries to accomplish. As a result of this defeat of the Muslims, many of them migrated and resettled in the region of Morocco as Spain gradually became intolerant towards them. Among the many Muslim families that resettled in Morocco was the family of Leo Africanus, whose original name was Al-Hasan ibn-Muhammad al-Waezaz al-Fasi. Leo's uncle was a prominent individual and from time to time served in a diplomatic capacity and traveled a significant amount in the region. Leo accompanied his uncle on some of his tours which gave him the opportunity to become well informed about the peoples and countries that he visited and also developed in him the interest for additional travel. Leo was regarded as a highly educated individual, and he was also, from an early time, conversant in several languages including Arabic, Spanish and Italian.

Around 1520, as fate would have it, Leo was on a boat traveling in the Mediterranean when it was captured by a group of Christian pirates. Piracy was a common phenomenon at the time and the victims, if they were not killed, were sold into slavery. Fortunately for Leo, he was neither killed nor sold into slavery. His captors realized that they had encountered an individual who was quite extraordinary—his fluency in several languages and his knowledge of many lands were recognized valuable assets. He was, therefore, presented to the Pope who, at the time, was Leo X. The Pope, also recognizing the valuable attributes of the captive, treated him with dignity and honor, granted him his freedom, and provided him with a pension so that he could remain close to the papal court and pursue scholarly interests. Eventually, the Pope even succeeded in converting his learned guest to Christianity and bestowed upon him the name of Leo. During his stay in Rome, Leo Africanus completed the book that would make him famous in history. The book, entitled *The History and Description of Africa and the Notable Things Therein Contained*, was completed in 1526 in Arabic and was first published in Italian in the 1550s. The book was soon translated into several other European languages and the English version, translated by John Pory, was published in 1600. Sadly, Pope Leo X died three years before the completion of Leo Africanus' work. After the death of the Pope who had shown so much kindness and generosity to him, Leo Africanus was relegated to lesser status and, eventually, it is said that he returned to Morocco where he reembraced the Islamic faith and died in 1552.

His book, however, remained the most valuable account about Africa for the next three hundred years.

Leo's account about the Western Sudan is based upon his visit there a few years before he was captured by the pirates. According to Robert Brown, the editor and commentator of John Pory's English version of Leo's book, Leo probably traveled to the Western Sudan between 1513 and 1515. Leo had traveled there in the company of his uncle, who had been sent by the Sultan of Fez on a diplomatic mission to the ruler of Timbuktu. Leo described the land and the peoples of the Western Sudan as he saw them firsthand.

In the Western Sudan Leo traveled through fifteen territories that he defined as kingdoms. These were not all independent kingdoms, however, but came under the domination of three kings, who reigned over Timbuktu, Borno and Gaoga. Some of the kingdoms, especially those under the control of Timbuktu, must have been a part of the empire of Songhay which was the dominant imperial power in the Western Sudan at the time; Timbuktu was one of its major cities. All these fifteen territories were, according to Leo, Bilad as-Sudan (country of the blacks). He listed these as (equivalent modern names are in parentheses) Gualata (Walata), Ghinea (Guinea), Melli (Mali), Tombotu (Timbuktu), Gago (Gao), Gober (Gobir), Agades, Cano (Kano), Cafena (Katsina), Zegzeg, Zamfara, Guangara (Wangara), Borno, Gaogo and Nube. The Songhay language was the common language in many of these regions. While these were the only black states that he visited, he acknowledged the existence of many more that were known and frequented by other Africans. The kingdoms that he visited were generally located along the Niger river. Most of these kingdoms were adjacent to one another. These territories, he stated, were connected in the trans-Saharan trade route that extended all the way to Cairo in Egypt. The journey to Egypt, he described, was very long and occasionally safe and free of danger. However, in general, traveling through the desert was always a challenge due to lack of water and the risks of being attacked by hostile inhabitants. He described the land of the black Africans along the Niger as being abundant in cattle, corn, cucumbers, onions, fruits and herbs.

Leo Africanus visited the Western Sudan when the power and control of ancient Mali had significantly diminished and its place was taken by the empire of Songhay. But some of the places that he visited were the same ones that were visited by Ibn Battuta in 1352-53 when Mali was at its peak. Therefore, a brief comparison is provided here to get a sense of the kind of changes that had taken place in the intervening years between the visits of Ibn Battuta and Leo Africanus in some of the towns and commercial centers that were visited by both of these men. The first such place is Walata, which in Ibn Battuta's time was the northernmost region under the control of Mali. Ibn Battuta had stayed there for fifty days. The inhabitants at that time were mostly Massufa Berbers. The town seemed to be a profitable center of trade inhabited by prosperous merchants. By the time of Leo's visit, the town had become poor. Its inhabitants were black West Africans whose language was Songhay, and it was part of the Songhay empire; the wealthy merchants had abandoned it in favor of Timbuktu during the reign of the conquering king of Songhay Sonni Ali in the 1470s. Leo described the people as very amicable towards strangers who visited their town. Another interesting comparison is that during the time of Ibn Battuta meat was quite abundant but during Leo's time it was very scarce. In general, Leo described the life of the people of Walata as quite miserable.

Mali, though considerably weakened by the time of Leo's visit, was nonetheless still prosperous and important enough to attract Leo. He visited its capital city, the exact name of which is not mentioned. According to Leo, the region of Mali was rich in corn, meat and cotton, and there were many merchants engaged in commerce. The inhabitants are described as being rich. The king was friendly and hospitable to strangers. In Mali, so stated Leo, there were many "temples, priests and professours." The people of this region surpassed all other black Africans, according to Leo, in wit, politeness, and good manners and hard work. However, after its conquest by the Songhay, the ruler of Mali had been subjected to some oppressive conditions. Ibn Battuta's observations about Mali were mixed. He was not too praiseworthy of the hospitality of the ruler. In Ibn Battuta's time there must have been more Berber communities present in Mali. Leo made no reference to their presence in Mali.

A most interesting comparison, based upon the writings of Ibn Battuta and Leo Africanus, has to be focused on Timbuktu. When the town was visited by Ibn Battuta in the 1350s, the town was controlled by the ruler of Mali. Originally founded as a camping stop by the nomads in the twelfth century, it gradually grew to become an important entrepot in the trans-Saharan trade. It became a terminus for caravans going to Morocco and Tunisia in particular. It was conquered by one of Sundiata's successors in the latter part of the 1200s, according to some sources. Other sources credit Mansa Musa's army for conquering the town. Mansa Musa had stopped there on his way back from Egypt in the 1320s and under his instructions a major mosque was built there. Ibn Battuta devotes only about half a page to this town. He stated that most of the inhabitants were Massufa Berbers, its governor's name was Farba Musa, and the grave of a renowned and distinguished poet and architect from Granada (more about him in a later chapter) was located in that city. He made no mention of the economy or the lifestyle of the town. However, by the time of Leo's visit, Timbuktu had undergone a major transformation in about a hundred and sixty years. Leo described Timbuktu as a town with many shops and traders, many of whom sold European cloth; a royal palace built by a Spanish architect; inhabitants who were exceedingly wealthy; abundant supplies of corn, cattle, and milk, although salt was in great shortage. Timbuktu had a thriving population of professional people like doctors, judges and religious functionaries who were well maintained and compensated from the ruler's treasury. The town was a major scholarly community where books and manuscripts were sold for more money than any other commodity. According to Leo Timbuktu minted its own gold coin. The people were gentle and of pleasant nature and temperament. During the sixteenth century, under the reigns of the kings of the Songhay empire Timbuktu experienced its golden age. It became a regionally renowned center of learning attracting scholars from many nearby countries who gathered at the town's most famous Sankore mosque-school complex.

Another important Western Sudanese town that both of our travelers visited was Gao. This town, located further east of Timbuktu along the Niger River, was initially established several centuries ago. It was the home of the Songhay people and became the nucleus from which the Songhay people embarked on their empire-building period during the late fourteenth and into the fifteenth centuries. Mansa Musa's army, according to the early Arabic sources, had conquered and made Gao a province within ancient Mali. A few modern authors place the date of Mali's conquest of Gao in the pre-Mansa Musa period. In any case, the city-state of Gao had prospered as a result of the trans-Saharan trade that passed through its territory carrying goods to and from Bornu and Egypt. The early rulers of Gao belonging to the Dia (or Ja) dynasty were among the earliest converts to Islam in the Western Sudan. Ibn Battuta described Gao as a large town and one of the most agreeable towns in Black Africa. He stayed there for about a month and found the town to be well-stocked with food supplies, rice, milk and fish in particular. Leo Africanus described the town in similar fashion as he had described Timbuktu; that is, Gao had many wealthy merchants and abundant food and water. He expressed his astonishment at the large quantity of goods that were brought into the town and how expensive and lavish these items were. Goods brought from Venice and Turkey were especially costly. Horses, spurs, bridles, and spices were all highly valued commodities. The most expensive commodity was salt. Away from Gao, he described the people of Songhay as lacking knowledge and ill-mannered.

Leo's description of travel through the Sahara Desert underscored the danger and high risk involved. He, more than Ibn Battuta, described the severity of the scarcity of water and the danger of death brought on by the travelers either getting lost or running short of water. He provided little information or description of the practical logistics of his own crossing of the Sahara. Ibn Battuta, on the other hand, gave more details about his crossing of the Sahara.

An interesting aspect of Leo Africanus' journey to West Africa and his account of it is that he is the first known outsider to have traveled to the Hausaland and provided a written account of that area. The cities of Gobir, Kano, Katsina, and Zamfara are some of the major cities of the Hausas that Leo visited. Like Ibn Battuta, Leo's work has been of immense value in the reconstruction of African history in the modern era.

The Sahara Desert, therefore, contrary to one's expectations, did not present an insurmountable obstacle for contacts between the lands to the north and the south of the desert. It witnessed more traffic over a longer period of time than other areas of Africa's interior. The introduction of the camel led to the establishment of regular and permanent links between the Western Sudan and North Africa. Outside of the Nile valley and the Horn of Africa, the peoples of the Western Sudan created and developed the next-oldest series of complex state and imperial systems. The trans-Saharan trade was one of the principal factors that made the growth of the Western Sudanese state system possible. The trans-Saharan trade, as we have learned from the accounts of Ibn Battuta and others, was dangerous but manageable after adequate preparation. The use of knowledgeable guides and camel drivers, usually from among the Tuareg or other Berber groups, was always of vital importance. The journey, preferably, had to be taken during the cooler months.

One of the most amazing episodes involving the crossing of the Sahara Desert occurred in the late sixteenth century, in the 1590s. This was the invasion of the Western Sudanese empire of Songhay by a Moroccan army. This probably is the first recorded crossing of the Sahara from either direction by a military force of one country against another. Sultan Ahmad of Morocco, enticed by the wealth of the Western Sudan, ordered an expedition that consisted of about four thousand men after the king of Songhay rejected the Moroccan demand to become subservient and refused to pay tribute to Morocco. The Moroccan force consisted of Arabs, Berbers, and many Spaniards, including the expedition's leader, Judar Pasha, a native of Granada. As described by Barbour, the "march across the desert was terrible; the expedition, which took the route through Tinduf, Taghaza, and Taodeni, lost half its effectives before it reached the Niger, 135 days later" (1966). However, despite having a numerical advantage over the invading army, the army of the Songhay was defeated, partly because of the fact that the Moroccan army was armed with firearms such as muskets and some cannons. According to Fage, "8000 camels and 1000 horses were provided to transport the large amounts of ammunition, equipment, food and water which were necessary if the army were to arrive and fight successfully on the other side of the desert" (1978). It is said that Judar returned to Morocco with an enormous quantity of gold dust, slaves and other West African products. The conquest earned Sultan Ahmad of Morocco the titles of *Al-Mansur* (the Victorious) and *Al-Dhahabi* (the Golden) (Barbour, 1966).

By the end of the fifteenth century, the European presence along the West African coastline had been established. In the succeeding centuries, the development of the trans-Atlantic trade caused and led to the decline of the trans-Saharan trade to some extent. However, the trans-Saharan trade continued to remain an important factor in the geo-economics of the Western Sudan well into the nineteenth century. Camel caravans continue even to the present time to ply across the sands carrying loads of salt and other merchandise. Some of the early Europeans who reached the coast of West Africa and began the trans-Atlantic trade network had certainly heard accounts about the kingdoms in the interior of Western Sudan and about the trans-Saharan trade in gold. For the first time in the fourteenth century, European cartographers included reference to ancient Mali on their maps. A 1375 map (see p. 118) stated that the king of Mali was the noblest and the richest king in the land of Guinea. Thus there existed a strong desire on the part of numerous European explorers to reach the El Dorado of West Africa, especially the famed city of Timbuktu.

Nineteenth Century Exploration

It was not until the nineteenth century that several European explorers successfully made their way into the interior, some starting from the region of the Senegal and Gambia Rivers and others starting from the coast of North Africa. Some of these explorers left the most detailed accounts about the Western Sudan since the travels of Leo Africanus in the 1500s. A brief summary of the experiences and accounts of at least two of these prominent European explorers who crossed the Sahara Desert is provided below. Their accounts about the trans-Saharan trade as it was taking place during the nineteenth century, the descriptions of the major Western Sudanese cities such as Timbuktu, Jenne, Gao and others, and their discussions of the lifestyles of many of the peoples of the region are very noteworthy.

Two of the most renowned European travelers to the Western Sudan in the nineteenth century were Rene Caillie, a Frenchman, and Heinrich Barth, a German. Caillie came from a poor peasant background and from an early age became enamored with the idea of exploring the unknown regions of Africa. In particular, he became obsessed with the objective of reaching Timbuktu. After being rebuffed by the colonial officials of his native France, he joined up with a British-sponsored team of explorers from Sierra Leone to start realizing his dream. However, he soon concluded that if he were to succeed in reaching the mysterious city of Timbuktu, he would be better off striking out on his own. Also recognizing that as a Christian European he could run into much hostility in the interior, he concocted a plan to disguise himself as a Muslim who was attempting to make his way to the Holy City to perform the *hajj* (pilgrimage). In order to prepare for this adventure, he learned the Arabic language, familiarized himself with the Quran and the Muslim religion, and lived with a group of Moors in Mauritania (Ross, 1977). He set out in 1827 to reach his dream destination—the city of Timbuktu.

His disguise and pretense worked well, though he did not always receive warm hospitality. He encountered some Western Sudanese Muslims who robbed him and treated him nastily in some villages and towns. In other places, however, he encountered Muslims who provided him with food, lodging and guides, as well as cared for him while he was sick. After a difficult journey, he reached Timbuktu in 1828 and, needless to state, upon entering the city he experienced the most emotional moments of his life. After a few days' stay in the city, he continued his journey by crossing the Sahara Desert in the company of trans-Saharan trading caravans along the route that went to Morocco. He thus became the first European to have done what Ibn Battuta did in the 1350s, i.e. travel with a trading caravan across the Sahara. Thus Caillie's description of this segment of his journey is the most detailed one since Ibn Battuta's.

The second major European traveler to the Western Sudan, Heinrich Barth, undertook his journey in the 1850s, exactly five hundred years after Ibn Battuta. Barth came from a wealthier family than Caillie and had a strong academic background. His party started the journey from Tripoli in Libya and traveled across the Sahara and in West Africa for five years. Being a scholar-explorer, Barth left a detailed account of the journey in five volumes. For part of his journey he also found it wise to disguise as an Arab, although he did not hide his Christian identity.

From the accounts of these two explorers we get more details about the extreme difficulties involved in crossing the Sahara. Barth recounts the fear and the terror that he felt when separated from the caravan. After he himself became separated from his caravan and wandered about hopelessly for a while, he describes his reaction when he heard the distant sound of a camel that belonged to his separated caravan—"It was the most delightful music I ever heard in my life" (Barth, 1965). The author of the present experienced similar fright and terror when, in 1985, a group of us were lost in the desert for a few hours not far from Timbuktu. We had never rejoiced more than at the moment of sighting a herd of goats in the distance being shepherded by two little boys who guided us to their village where the elders guided us to the banks of the Niger River.

Caillie provides more vivid accounts of the misery associated with thirst, hunger and illness while crossing the desert. People sometimes were driven to drinking the urine of the camel to quench their thirst and biting their own flesh in times of great hunger. Sandstorms and extreme heat were also other major hazards. Sometimes travelers would have to wait for weeks and months before being able to find a caravan. Often peoples through whose territories the caravans passed expected to be paid tolls and protection money. Traveling during the night was a common practice. Caravans ranged in size from a few hundred camels to a few thousand camels. Neither Barth nor Caillie encountered very large caravans such as the one referred to by Ibn Khaldun in the 1300s which had consisted of twelve thousand camels. James Jackson, an Englishman, who lived in Morocco for around 16 years around the turn of the 19th century, reported the perishing in 1805 of one caravan of nearly two thousand camels due to lack of water.

Both Caillie and Barth describe that the salt and the gold trade was still very important and valuable in the nineteenth century as it had been in the previous ones. Salt was a rare and valued commodity in the Western Sudan. To be served food with salt in it was, in the words of Caillie, "A tremendous and generous treat...salt was literally gold" (quoted in Ross, 1977). Barth reports that salt was sometimes even more valued than gold. According to Jackson, in the early 1800s, commodities that were in demand in the Western Sudan also included a variety of textiles, spices, a variety of beads, and tobacco. Gold, slaves and a variety of animal products such as ivory dominated the exports of the Western Sudan.

Finally, Caillie and Barth had somewhat different observations about the fabled city of Timbuktu. Caillie found it to be a dull city with little activity. There were only a handful of shops doing business in the late 1820s when he passed through it. This is how Caillie described the city:

> At length, we arrived safely at Timbuktu, just as the sun was touching the horizon. Now I saw this capital of the Sudan, to reach which had so long been the object of my wishes. On entering this mysterious city...I experienced an indescribable satisfaction....I looked around and found that the sight before me did not answer my expectations. I had formed a totally different idea of the grandeur and wealth of Timbuktu. The city presented, at first view, nothing but a mass of ill-looking houses, built of earth....I found the city neither so large nor so populous as I had expected. Its commerce is not so considerable as fame has reported...the market was a desert. (Quoted in Killingray, 1973)

Barth, on the other hand, reported the following in the 1850s:

Almost the whole life of the city is based upon foreign commerce....In all this commerce gold forms the chief staple, although the whole amount of the precious metal exported from this city appears to be exceedingly small, if compared with a European standard.... (Barth, 1965)

Thus, the trans-Saharan trade served to link the Western Sudan with the outside world for at least two thousand years. The trade was significantly responsible for the growth of the early states and empires and for the introduction of the Islamic civilization and its influence in the region. The trans-Saharan trade did not disappear with the growth of the trans Atlantic trade, as is often suggested. The trans-Saharan trade remained fairly important until the end of the nineteenth century.

CHAPTER III

ISLAM: THE INTERNATIONAL CONNECTION

Introduction

The preceding chapter detailed the trade connection between the Western Sudan and North Africa. While we do not known for certain the final destinations of the exports from the Western Sudan during these early centuries, there is a high probability that some of these exports, especially gold, ivory and slaves ended up in countries beyond North Africa such as Spain, Arabia, Syria and Iraq, all of which were part of the Islamic world. If the Western Sudanese exports reached markets in Christian Europe between the eighth and the fifteenth centuries, these are not directly evidenced in the early records. Evidence from the early accounts indicates that the Western Sudan's strongest commercial connections were with the Islamic countries to the north and non-Islamic African states to the south. As elaborated in the last chapter, the early sources have left many accounts about the commercial connections between the Western Sudan and the Islamic world to the north. References in the early Arabic sources to the trade between the Western Sudanese peoples and other African peoples to the south are quite few. But there is no doubt that the trade relations with the lands to the south must have been strong because some of the goods exported from the Western Sudan, such as slaves, ivory and kola nuts, originated in the southern kingdoms. For the period after the fifteenth century, accounts by European traders and travelers provide us with more details about the coastal African states' relations with the Western Sudanese kingdoms and peoples. Thus, for ancient Mali as well as other Western Sudanese states, the international trade linkages were the strongest with the Islamic world.

While we have much information from the early Arabic sources about ancient Mali's and Western Sudan's commercial connections with the Islamic world, information regarding their political or diplomatic relations is very minimally referenced in these early sources, especially for the period before the nineteenth century. Again, the few cases or instances of diplomatic and international political relations of the Western Sudanese kingdoms that are mentioned in the early sources inform us that these occurred primarily with the Islamic world. These small number of documented early cases are briefly described later in this chapter.

In addition to the commercial and political connections that ancient Mali and Western Sudan had with the Islamic world, there were also intellectual and scholarly ties that developed between the Western Sudanese and the wider Islamic world. For wherever Islam had spread, it also introduced the culture of literacy. Thus, important centers of learning evolved in several major Western Sudanese cities such as Timbuktu, Gao, and Jenne which attracted Islamic scholars from numerous Islamic states. Some of these are discussed in detail later on in this chapter.

Thus, the religion and culture of Islam played a significant part in linking ancient Mali and other Western Sudanese kingdoms to the international system of the period. The Islamic connection contributed and facilitated the development of strong commercial, intellectual and some diplomatic ties between ancient Mali and other kingdoms. A brief description about the origin and the spread of Islam to the Western Sudan and ancient Mali is in order.

Origin and Expansion of Islam

Within the first decade after the death of the Prophet in A.D. 632, the successive Arab *Caliphs* (leaders of the newly established Islamic state) embarked on expansionist policies that were to permanently change the demographic, religious and political map of many of the lands between Morocco to the west and Afghanistan to the east. The Arab armies, in a series of incredibly successful campaigns, conquered a vast number of territories that previously formed parts of the Byzantine and Sasanian empires. They conquered major cities like Damascus, Jerusalem and Cairo in the process. The Islamic state had been converted into an empire and gradually the Islamic religion transformed from being an Arab creed to a universal faith embracing peoples of many diverse backgrounds.

Muslims consider Islam to be the last of the revealed religions and Prophet Muhammad to have been the "seal of the Prophets." Muhammad was born in A.D. 570 among the *Quraysh* tribe of Arabia. He was orphaned from an early age and was brought up by his uncle. As a young man, he became employed to work in some of the trading caravans that traveled from the *Hijaz* (western part of the Arabian peninsula) to other parts of Arabia and the Middle East. In his early twenties he married a wealthy woman, Khadija, who was much older than he. He received his mission of prophethood in the year A.D. 610, at the age of forty, while he was meditating in the mountains near Mecca. A spirit, believed by Muslims to have been angel Gabriel, communicated to Muhammad that God, Allah, had designated him as His apostle. For the next twenty-two years, Muhamamad received, through the angel Gabriel, divine messages that form the foundation of the Islamic faith. These revelations concerned not only religious matters, but also provided injunctions and guidance related to family relations, economic practices, relations with non-believers, justice and judicial matters, relations between the genders, and matters of politics.

As Muhammad went about preaching and teaching the new faith in Mecca, he quickly ran into opposition from the Meccan establishment who feared that Muhammad's success would threaten and possibly end their power and influence. Consequently, Muhammad's life was in danger; therefore, following divine instructions, he left or migrated from Mecca in A.D. 622 for the town of Medina, about two hundred miles to the north, where he was better received. Muhammad's migration to Medina, known as the *Hijra* or *Hejira*, marks the beginning of the Islamic calendar.

Over the next ten years there took place several wars between Muhammad's community and the Meccans. These wars ultimately ended with Mecca being conquered by Muhammad's followers in A.D. 630 Muhammad, however, continued to live in Medina until his death in A.D. 632. His tomb is located in that city up to the present time. A few years after his death, the revelations that he had received were compiled and written down into one collection, the Quran. According to the Islamic beliefs, every word in the Quran is a word of Allah as delivered through Prophet Muhammad. Neither Prophet Muhammad nor any other human being is regarded as the author of the Quran. The Quran, in addition to providing a fairly detailed code of conduct by which the followers must live, contains many passages that confirm the revelations sent to previous Prophets; exhortations for humanity to heed the word of God; and warnings to humanity of dire consequences resulting from not following the revelations.

The principal beliefs of Islam, which means submission to the will of God, are acceptance of Allah as One God and

Mohammad as His Prophet, recitation of *salat* (prayers) five times each day during prescribed hours, fasting from dawn to dusk during the month of *Ramadhan,* giving of the *zakat* (tithe), and undertaking the performance of the *hajj* (pilgrimage) at least once in a lifetime. Beyond the fulfillment of these principal beliefs, the followers are expected to live according to the *Shariah*, the laws and injunctions prescribed in the Quran. The *hadith* and the *sunnah*, the sayings, practices and traditions of Prophet Muhammad, provide additional guidance and requirements for the followers of Islam on how to live their lives.

Soon after the death of the Prophet Muhammad, Islam experienced a schism which has persisted throughout its history. The schism is manifested in the existence of the *Sunni* and *Shia (Shiite)* branches of Islam. A vast majority of the Muslims throughout the world and throughout Islamic history have been followers of the *Sunni* branch. A major cause that led to the schism was the question of succession to the Prophet. One school of thought selected Prophet Muhammad's successors, *Caliphs,* from among the close companions of the Prophet through a process of consensus. This school became the *Sunni* branch. A minority believed that the line of succession must remain hereditary and within the family of Prophet Muhammad through his daughter Fatima. This school became the *Shia* branch. The people of Iran and the followers of the Aga Khan, the Ismailis, constitute the largest groups of *Shia* in the modern world.

Expansion of Islam in the Western Sudan

As pointed out earlier, Egypt was the first African country conquered by the Arab forces in A.D. 639. By the end of the seventh century, the Arab/Islamic forces had subdued the last of the major opposition put up by the Berbers of North and Northwest Africa and the remaining outposts of the Byzantine Empire in northern Africa. Northern Africa was permanently brought under the banner of Islam. While some of the Berber tribes embraced Islamic religion quite early on after their conquest and participated in the Islamic armies, many other Berber tribes resisted conversion to Islam for years to come. Thus, Islamization of the Berbers and much of the lands in northern Africa that they occupied took approximately two centuries. Islam and Arabic gradually replaced Christianity and Latin in North Africa. Once assimilated into the Islamic culture and civilization, many Berbers contributed politically, economically, militarily and culturally to the evolution of the Islamic civilization. North Africa and Spain witnessed the rise and fall of numerous Berber Islamic dynasties. North Africa witnessed the establishment and growth of new major Islamic cities such as Kairawan, Fez and Marrakesh. Many Berber tribes became major proselytizing agents on behalf of Islam. They played a crucial part in introducing the message of Islam to the Western Sudanese. The expansion of Islam into North Africa stimulated the southward migrations into and across the Sahara by many Berbers.

The earliest Arabic sources that discuss the spread of Islam to the Western Sudan include the accounts of Al-Masudi (late tenth century), Al-Muhallabi (late tenth century), Al-Bakri (eleventh century), Al-Nazir (twelfth century), and a few others. These sources inform us about the presence and settlements of Muslim communities in several Western Sudanese towns; provide some insights into the relationship between Muslims and non-Muslim Western Sudanese; describe the earliest conversions of the Western Sudanese rulers to Islam; and provide details about some of the wars and conflicts that occurred in the Western Sudan.

From the accounts of these early Arabic authors, it is established that traders were the first to introduce Islam into the Western Sudan. Most of these Muslim traders were from various Berber tribes. Some came from as far as Egypt and Ifriqiya (modern Tunisia). These Muslim communities were present in numerous Western Sudanese towns such as Audaghost and Kumbi Saleh that were linked in the trans-Saharan trade network. The early accounts inform us that the Muslims lived entirely in separate towns or in separate quarters of the Western Sudanese towns. Ibn Hawqal (tenth century) wrote that the Muslim traders who settled in the kingdom of ancient Ghana were accorded a distinct and somewhat autonomous status whereby they were governed by their own judges (Saad, 1983). The most detailed such early account is that of Al-Bakri (eleventh century). Al-Bakri compiled fairly detailed account about the ancient empire of Ghana by gathering information from travelers. Regarding Islam in Ghana, Al-Bakri stated the following: "The city of Ghana consists of two towns situated on a plain. One of these towns, which is inhabited by Muslims, is large and possesses twelve mosques, in one of which they assemble for the Friday prayer. There are salaried imams (those who lead in prayers and administer the mosque) and muezzins (the prayer callers), as well as jurists and scholars" (Levtzion & Hopkins, 1981). He further stated that many of the high ranking officials in ancient Ghana's administration were

Muslims including the chief treasurer. Regarding one king, King Basi, Al-Bakri wrote that "He led a praiseworthy life on account of his love of justice and friendship for the Muslims."

There are no clear indications as to the efforts, if any, that were made by these Muslim merchants in the ninth and tenth centuries at converting the Western Sudanese natives to Islam. Trimingham (1970) suggests that these traders were little interested in spreading Islam at first.

The first Western Sudanese ruler to have converted to Islam is said to have been the ruler of Takrur, which was the most important Western Sudanese kingdom located along the Senegal River. Again, this bit of information comes to us from the account of Al-Bakri. According to Al-Bakri, Warjabi (also referred to as War Dyabi), the king of Takrur, converted to Islam sometime in the early eleventh century. He is said to have implemented Islamic law in his kingdom before his death around A.D. 1040 (Levtzion & Hopkins, 1981). Takrur and its neighboring towns Awlil and Sila, according to the early sources, were important commercial centers and were linked with both the North African as well as other Western Sudanese trading towns. The people of Takrur became very active missionaries of Islam and played an important part in spreading Islam to many other groups in West Africa.

Eleventh century also saw the spread of Islam among the Soninke people of ancient Ghana. Conversion of the people of ancient Ghana was probably the direct result of the Almoravid conquest of the Western Sudanese state in the 1070s. The Almoravid conquest represents the first time that Islam was spread into Western Sudan by means of force. Ancient Ghana declined as a result of this invasion, and its people, the Soninke, are said to have embraced Islam *en masse* under duress (Trimingham, 1970). Eventually, the Soninke Muslim merchants became quite active in spreading Islam to many other peoples in the Western Sudan.

The Western Sudanese people around the bend of the Niger River were also among the earliest West Africans to convert to Islam. In this region, the ruler of the town of Kawkaw had accepted Islam in the early eleventh century. According to Al-Idrisi, the king of Kawkaw was quite wealthy and powerful and had the Friday *khutba* (sermon) delivered in his own name as opposed to the name of a distant *caliph* or any other ruler. Another town, Kanim, is recorded in the early accounts to have embraced Islam in early 1100. Thus, by the end of the twelfth century, Islam had been firmly planted in the savannah region of the Western Sudan. Next, we examine the specific circumstances of the spread of Islam in the empire of Mali.

Expansion of Islam in Ancient Mali

According to certain oral traditions maintained by the Malinke *griots*, the very origin of the founders of ancient Mali, the Keita clan, is linked to Islamic roots. According to these traditions, the progenitor of the Keita clan was Bilali, a former African slave who had become a close companion of the Prophet Muhammad (Conrad, 1985). These traditions state that one of the sons of Bilali left Mecca and settled in Mali and became the founder of the clan from which came Sundiata, the great hero of the Malinke people who defeated the "evil" Sumanguru and set the stage for the development of the empire of ancient Mali. Thus, as per these traditions, Sundiata and all of his predecessors were Muslims from a fairly early time. According to Conrad (1985), there are other episodes that occurred in early Islamic history in Mecca that were absorbed or assimilated into the Malinke legends focusing on their Islamic origin.

The earliest written reference to the spread of Islam in ancient Mali is provided by Al-Bakri. Al-Bakri not only mentioned that the king of Malal (acknowledged by most modern historians to mean Mali) was a Muslim, but he also described the circumstances which resulted in the conversion of the first Muslim king of ancient Mali. According to Al-Bakri's account, the land of Malal at one time had been suffering from severe drought. The king described the suffering and the hardship that his people were experiencing to a visiting Muslim who was a guest of the king. The Muslim guest responded by urging the king to accept Allah and the message of the Prophet Muhammad and to recite the Islamic prayer. He assured the king that if he embraced Islam, God would respond favorably to his prayers and end the drought. After much urging, the king agreed, and on the following Friday the Muslim visitor initiated the king to Muslim prayers. The following day abundant rain fell. The drought was over. Thereafter, the king, his descendants and the nobles became devout Muslims (Levtzion & Hopkins, 1981). Al-Bakri does not give us the name of this first Muslim king of Mali. Ibn Khaldun in the late fourteenth century mentioned that the first king of Mali to embrace Islam was Baramandana. The masses of the people, however, did not convert to the new faith, and Islam is said to have remained for a long time the religion of the ruling elite in ancient Mali as well as in numerous other Western Sudanese kingdoms.

Concerning Sundiata, the great founding father of the empire of Mali, there are differing versions in the oral traditions as to whether he was Muslim. Some traditions suggest that he was a devout Muslim, but other traditions present him as a practitioner of traditional African religion. A reference in the account of Ibn Battuta (1350s) noted that Sundiata (referred to as Saraq Jata) was converted to Islam. Trimingham (1962) suggests that Sundiata was "almost certainly brought up as a pagan." The *Mansas* of Mali who succeeded Sundiata were, without doubt, Muslims, for a few of them went on the pilgrimage to Mecca (the *Mansas* are discussed in more detail in a later chapter). From the middle of the thirteenth century Islam had become well entrenched at least at the level of the ruling class and the urban merchant class.

The early records do not provide us much information regarding the extent or the day-to-day practice of Islam in ancient Mali. Our only eyewitness account about the practice of Islam in ancient Mali covers part of the fourteenth century and comes from Ibn Battuta, who spent about two years traveling through ancient Mali during the 1350s. His observations are quite noteworthy and are briefly described below.

Ibn Battuta refers to a strong presence of the Ibadi sect of the Sunni branch in the Western Sudan. The Ibadis had rebelled against the early leaders of both the Sunni and the Shia branches of Islam claiming that the leader of Islam (*Caliph*) must be elected by the Muslim community at large. The Ibadis became a major force in Oman and then in North Africa from where they spread to the Western Sudan by the ninth century. The impression left by Ibn Battuta is that the Ibadis were mostly lighter-skinned and of mostly Berber background. They are characterized as highly devoted and quite zealous. In some of the towns that Ibn Battuta visited during his travels through Mali, he sent messages out in advance to some of these "white" residents to make arrangements for his lodging.

When Ibn Battuta arrived in the capital city of ancient Mali, he lodged in the "white" quarter of the town. He reports how well he was received by the *qadi* (a Muslim judge), who was black and had been on the pilgrimage. On several other occasions, Ibn Battuta mentions being received by or meeting *qadis*. This clearly indicates that Islamic law or at least aspects of it were applied in ancient Mali. He also observed that the people of the capital city of Mali were meticulous about observing the prayer hours and attended congregational prayers with great frequency. Friday prayers attracted large numbers of people dressed in their cleanest whites. The people were, he described, diligent in learning and memorizing the Quran. The children were strongly disciplined if they slacked in learning the Quran.

Ibn Battuta's stay in Mali extended through the two major festivals of Islam—the feast at the end of the month-long fasting period during Ramadhan, and the festival of sacrifice. On these occasions the king joined the general populace in saying the prayers. According to Ibn Battuta, the king was escorted by the notables and the flag-bearers in a procession to the site of the prayers where the king performed his ablutions in a specially pitched tent before joining the congregation. Upon completion of the prayers, the king listened to the sermon (Levtzion, 1980). Ibn Battuta describes some of the pageantry that took place on these days following the prayers:

> On these days the sultan takes his seat on the *pempi* after the midafternoon prayer. The armour-bearers bring in magnificent arms—quivers of gold and silver swords ornamented with gold and with golden scabbards, gold and silver lances and crystal maces. At his head stand four amirs driving off the flies, having in their hands silver ornaments resembling saddle-stirrups. The commanders, qadi, and preacher sit in their usual places. The interpreter Dugha comes with his four wives and his slave-girls, who are about hundred in number. They are wearing beautiful robes, and on their heads they have gold and silver fillets....(The Dugha) plays on instrument made of reeds...and chants a poem in praise of the sultan, recalling his battles and deeds of valour. The women and girls sing along with him and play with bows....Thereupon the sultan orders a gift to be presented to Dugha and he is given a purse containing two hundred *mithqals* (about fifty grams) of gold dust....(1969)

Some of these rituals, according to Ibn Battuta, were practices from the pre-Islamic times. Ibn Battuta also commented upon some of the qualities of the black people of Mali that he found to be admirable.

They are seldom unjust, and have a greater abhorrence of injustice than any other people. Their sultan shows no mercy to anyone who is guilty of the least act of it. There is complete security in their country. Neither traveller nor inhabitant in it has anything to fear from robbers or men of violence. They do not confiscate the property of any white man who dies in their country, even if it be uncounted wealth. On the contrary, they give it into the charge of some trustworthy person among the whites, until the rightful heir takes possession of it . (1969)

It is interesting to note that this last point made by Ibn Battuta confirms that this practice of returning a deceased foreigner's belongings to his rightful heir had been in existence for many decades. An account written in the 1230s, over a hundred years before Ibn Battuta, stated the following: "My wife's father died in the land of the Sudan and the property which he left arrived at the city of Fez. We found among it a pouch of gold dust." This pouch bore the name of the individual who had sent some merchandise with the deceased man (Levtzion & Hopkins, 1981).

The qualities of the people of Mali that Ibn Batutta found to be negative and abhorrent were the practices of women going about their chores in partial nudity, the eating of dog and donkey meat, the people's custom of putting dust or ashes on their heads as a sign of respect and the practice of cannibalism among a certain tribe. As Ibn Battuta continued his journey through Mali after his stay at the capital, he did not describe much more about the practice of Islam except that he met with some *qadis* in some of the towns and he also encountered several individuals who had performed the pilgrimage.

Another interesting point to note about Islam in ancient Mali is that, according to a few fourteenth century sources, the *Maliki* school of Islamic law had become dominant and widespread in the region. Islam has as its sources for religious law the Quran, the *Hadith* (the sayings and practices of the Prophet Muhammad), and four different schools of legal interpretations. These schools of law started to develop during the period between the seventh and the ninth centuries in different parts of the Islamic world (Arabia, Iraq and Egypt). These four schools of legal interpretations of Islamic law are the Hanafi, the Hanbali, the Shafii and the Maliki. Each of these schools became important in different parts of the

Islamic world. These schools differed with each other on matters of interpretation of the Islamic law. The Maliki school, which became widespread in the Western Sudan, emphasized that in addition to the Quran and the *hadith*, the opinions of the scholars of Medina should be considered and incorporated in the formulation of the Islamic law.

As mentioned earlier, during these early centuries and about the mid-1800s, Islam remained a religion of the minority of the people of the Western Africa. It became primarily the religion of the royal clans, the urban dwellers and the merchant class. Those common people who were followers are said to have been attracted to Islam because of its potential as a healing force. People sometimes embraced Islam believing that the power of Islamic charms and amulets would cure their illnesses. But in general, the masses of the people of ancient Mali are said to have continued to believe in and practice their traditional religions. A notable case cited in the early sources refers to the inhabitants of the gold-producing region. It is stated that whenever the rulers of Mali tried to impose the religion of Islam upon these people, they reacted and resisted by refusing to mine the gold. The rulers of Mali then left them alone and seemed contented as long as the tributes were paid in gold. Fage (1978) suggests that one important reason that Islam did not gain widespread acceptance among many Western Sudanese during these early centuries was due to the rejection by the Western Sudanese of the idea that there was one God for both the kinsmen and the foreigners. This proposition, according to Fage, was regarded as "treasonable." At the same time, however, there were towns in ancient Mali, most notably Timbuktu, that are said to have been even more Islamic than some of the cities of North Africa or the Middle East (Saad, 1983). The *Tarikh al-Fattash,* the seventeenth century Western Sudanese chronicle, mentioned one particular town in the middle of ancient Mali, Diaba, which was so Islamic that even the king did not enter it because the king's authority was subordinate there. This town is said to have served as a refuge from the king's oppression and it was under the authority of its *qadi* (Islamic judge) (Levtzion, 1980).

Community of Scholars

Encouragement of the pursuit of knowledge was one of the major factors that contributed to the emergence of Islam as a major world civilization. The golden age of Islam came, in part, due to the contributions of a vast number of Muslim scholars who were in the forefront of the advancement of knowledge both in the sacred as well as the secular disciplines. This emphasis upon the pursuit of knowledge drew inspiration from both the Quran as well as the *hadith* of the Prophet Muhammad. Some of the sayings attributed to the Prophet include "The pen of the scholar is mightier than the sword of the martyr" and "Seek knowledge from the cradle to the grave."

Thus, a major impact of Islam upon the Western Sudan was the introduction of literacy and the development of an intellectual and a scholarly community which helped connect the Western Sudan with the wider Islamic world. After trade, scholarly activity was perhaps the next most important endeavor that interconnected Muslims from diverse parts of the Islamic world. In fact, in Islam, a very strong association existed between trade and scholarship. In the Western Sudan, extensive interactions took place between many North African, Egyptian, and Western Sudanese scholars, especially after the fifteenth century. Probably the earliest instance of the use of writing by a Western Sudanese is the case of a king of ancient Ghana who corresponded with a ruler in a region of Morocco. Al-Nazir, writing in the 1130s, mentioned that he had seen a letter written by the king of Ghana to the Almoravid leader Yusuf b. Tashfin (Levtzion & Hopkins, 1981). Another source informs us that after Islam had spread in ancient Ghana, many schools were established there.

The Islamic religious school or *madarasa* was often a concomitant part of an Islamic mosque. The Islamic culture placed much value in teaching the reading skills because in order to be able to practice the religion more faithfully, the follower must be able to read the Quran. Therefore, learning to read, recite and memorize the Quran were at the core of the basic education in the Islamic model. Gradually, the *madarasas* evolved into more advanced institutions where complex subjects such as theological sciences, the *hadith*, history, geography, mathematics, logic, Arabic grammar, philosophy and physical sciences became part of the curriculum. Major centers of learning developed in all corners of the Islamic world—Egypt, Iraq, Tunisia, Morocco, Spain, Iran and eventually in the Western Sudan as well.

For the period prior to the fourteenth century, the extent and the progress of the *madarasa*-based learning in the Western Sudan is largely undocumented. A few accounts in the early sources make references that allude to the existence of scholarly communities in some of the Western Sudanese towns during the fourteenth century during the period of Mansa Musa and his successors. Ibn Battuta observed that in Walata, which was part of the empire of Mali at the time but whose residents were mostly Massufa Berbers, the people studied books of law in addition to memorizing the Quran. The people of another town in Mali, Zagha, that Ibn Battuta visited showed great love and enthusiasm for study. Dia, another town within the empire of ancient Mali, also enjoyed a reputation as a scholarly town during the fourteenth century. However, Ibn Battuta made no mention of any organized scholarly activity in the capital city of Mali where he stayed for many months. Neither did he mention about any scholarly activity in Timbuktu, although there is a tradition that recorded that an Arabian migrant who settled in Timbuktu in the 1320s found the "town virtually teeming with Sudani scholars" (Saad, 1983). In fact, it is said that this immigrant, Abd al-Rahman al-Tamimi, discovered that the scholars in Timbuktu surpassed him in learning, and as a result he is said to have gone to Fez to study more and then returned to Timbuktu (Levtzion, 1980). Therefore, the fourteenth century rulers of ancient Mali are given credit to some extent for having promoted the development of a scholarly tradition in the Western Sudan that would culminate in the golden age of the medieval Western Sudanese scholarship in the sixteenth and the seventeenth centuries.

Mansa Musa, in particular, promoted scholarship and intellectual interactions between the people of Mali and other Islamic kingdoms, principally in North Africa and Egypt, by sending some Malians to study in Fez, Morocco; by patronizing scholars within his own realm; and by inviting learned individuals to come to Mali. These points are discussed in detail in a later chapter.

The Islamic tradition of learning and scholarship, which first took root during the period of ancient Ghana and which reached a level of recognizable maturity during the period of ancient Mali, reached its most distinguished and proliferous stage during the period of ancient Songhay in the sixteenth century. Several Western Sudanese towns became major centers of learning, most notably Timbuktu, Jenne, Gao and Walata, all of which in the fourteenth century were within the borders of ancient Mali. To the east of ancient Mali were located the Hausa city-states such as Kano, Zaria and Katsina which also developed significant scholarly traditions in later centuries.

Several factors are recognized to have contributed to the emergence and growth of a deep-rooted tradition of scholarship in the Western Sudanese towns. The Islamic influence was certainly most influential, for it introduced a culture of literacy. Arabic became the principal language of communication among the community of scholars which consisted of intellectuals from diverse ethnic backgrounds. However, the introduction of literacy in itself was not a sufficient condition. The urban character of the Western Sudanese societies provided an environment in which individuals could gain fame, positions of power, and wealth through scholarly pursuits. The Western Sudanese scholarly tradition was predominantly an urban tradition (Cissoko, 1975). The presence of scholars from other parts of the Islamic world, mainly from North Africa and Egypt, also played a very important part by introducing scholarly works from their respective regions and by establishing their own *madarasas*. Often the scholars of these towns were acknowledged to be among the most notable citizens. In some towns they formed part of the ruling elite or played a prominent part in the administration of justice. Al-Bakri informs us that as early as the eleventh century, the king of ancient Ghana preferred to employ Muslims in key positions of his administration. In the words of Al-Bakri, "The king's interpreters, the official in charge of his treasury and the majority of his ministers are Muslims" (Levtzion & Hopkins, 1981). As pointed out earlier, there were certain towns in ancient Mali that were so strongly controlled by Islamic judges that even the king had to respect their power and influence. Finally, the presence of a wealthy merchant class in these towns had a very favorable impact on the growth of scholarship. Trade in books was profitable and that meant that there was a steady supply of manuscripts from North Africa and Egypt into the Western Sudanese towns. The wealthy merchants also patronized and endowed the scholars. Scholars are also said to have been well compensated by the town rulers.

The names of only a handful of scholars who became prominent in ancient Mali during the fourteenth century have survived. These included Muhammad Al-Kaburi, Sidi Yaiya, Al-Abbas Mandawiyyu, Sissi Kuri and Turi Kuri. Some of these left intellectual and familial legacies that contributed to the enhancement of the Western Sudanese scholarly tradition.

The fifteenth and sixteenth centuries witnessed a proliferation of scholars and scholarly works in the Western Sudanese towns, especially in Timbuktu and Jenne. In a very detailed piece of research and analysis, Saad (1983) has brought to light the extensive depth of the scholarly tradition that evolved in Timbuktu during these centuries. Saad identifies and enumerates a vast number of scholars, too many to list, who were involved in scholarly pursuit and describes the chains of transmission of knowledge that developed in the Timbuktu region. Some of the most prominent ones included Mahmud Umar Aqit (1463-1563), Muhammad Baghayoughu (1523-1594), Abul Abbas Ahmad b. Muhammad Said (died 1568), and, the most celebrated of them all, Ahmed Baba (1556-1627), whose writings had achieved fame in North Africa and Egypt as well. According to Dubois (1896), "An extraordinary number of pupils attended his lectures, and questions of the gravest importance were submitted to him by the magistracy, his decision always being treated as final." More than thirty of his works have survived. He wrote about subjects as varied as astronomy, slavery, the Quran, jurisprudence, ethnography and biographies.

At the height of the golden age of the medieval Western Sudanese scholarly tradition, Timbuktu alone is said to have had as many as a hundred and fifty *madarasa*. The town had become a regional center of learning. The pedagogical model that evolved in the Western Sudan was, needless to say, the teacher- or scholar-centered. Attendance at these *madarasa* is said to have been free of charge. Interest and dedication to learning seemed to be the requisite criteria. The scholars' erudition, specialization and delivery style seemed to have determined the size of their following. It was not uncommon for students to study under several different scholars. Some of the more successful scholars even became revered by the general populace.

Many scholars seemed to have maintained large collections of books in their personal libraries. Works of numerous authors from as far away as Syria have been identified to have been among the collections of these Western Sudanese scholars. The celebrated scholar and author Ahmed Baba, who was taken across the Sahara Desert as a prisoner by the Moroccan army in the 1590s for his opposition to the Moroccan invasion of the empire of Songhay, complained to the sultan of Morocco, "Of all my friends I had the fewest books and yet when your soldiers despoiled me they took 1600 volumes" (DuBois, 1896). Ahmed Baba himself was a prolific writer. Heinrich Barth, who traversed the Sahara Desert and traveled through important regions of the Western Sudan in the 1850s, and whose writings provided the first detailed accounts of the Western Sudan since the time of Leo Africanus, more than three hundred years earlier, wrote the following about Ahmed Baba: "I have no hesitation in asserting that the work of Ahmed Baba will be one of the most important additions which the present age has made to the history of mankind, in a branch which was formerly unknown" (Barth, 1965, vol. 3).

The most famous center of learning that developed in the Western Sudan was Sankore in Timbuktu. It was, as it still is, an important quarter in the town of Timbuktu with the ancient mosque-school complex still in place. Sankore became the "main forum for interaction among scholars and literati" (Saad, 1983). This was especially the case in the sixteenth century when the Sankore quarter became the neighborhood with residences of the most distinguished scholars, including that of Ahmed Baba. The fame of the scholars based at Sankore became widespread. It was at Sankore that the famous chronicle of the Western Sudanese history *Tarikh as-Sudan* was produced by Abderahman al-Sadi. According to Bovill (1970), this work was first brought to the attention of the outside world by Heinrich Barth, who happened to have been shown a copy of it in 1853 during his travels through the Western Sudan.

Thus scholarship, along with trade, were the two major dimensions of the Western Sudanese kingdoms that became intimately interlinked with lands beyond the Western Sudan. And in both of these enterprises, the Western Sudan's connections were most extensive and strongest with the Islamic world. The early sources have enlightened us a good deal about the economic and scholarly links that existed between the Western Sudanese and the outside world during the time of the medieval empires. Very little information is provided by these early sources regarding the political and diplomatic relations that might have existed between ancient Mali or the other medieval empires and the outside world. The available information is synthesized in the following section.

Inter-State Relations

In this section an effort is made to understand the nature and levels of official contacts and interactions between ancient Mali in particular and other states and kingdoms. At the highest level, relations between states and kingdoms are expressed in visits and exchanges between the rulers of these states. Again, with respect to ancient Mali and the Western Sudanese kingdoms, their inter-state relations most frequently and most commonly were with the Islamic countries of North Africa, Egypt and Arabia.

With regard to ancient Mali, the conversion and Islamization of its rulers became an established fact after the middle of the 1200s, if not before. The Islamic identity of the kings who succeeded Sundiata is well attested to in the early sources. A number of these kings of ancient Mali and other Western Sudanese kingdoms traveled to Arabia in order to perform the pilgrimage. Two Western Sudanese kings who gained widespread fame as a result of their pilgrimage journeys were Mansa Musa of ancient Mali and Askiya Muhammad Toure of ancient Songhay. More detail about these pilgrimages is provided in a later chapter. The point to underscore here is that there were numerous kings of ancient Mali and other Western Sudanese kingdoms who traversed the Sahara Desert and traveled to and through at least a few Islamic countries. For the medieval centuries, there are no records of any reciprocal visits undertaken by the kings or the rulers of any North African kingdoms or of Egypt to the Western Sudan. The powerful rulers of various North African and Egyptian dynasties coveted the wealth of the Western Sudan, particularly gold, and occasionally sent military expeditions to the south, but they never seemed to have become interested enough to visit the lands to the south, either for economic or for political motives. Even after personal contacts were established, especially by some of the Egyptian rulers with the Western Sudanese rulers en route to Mecca, these contacts never culminated in any desire on the part of the Egyptian rulers to visit the *Bilad as-Sudan*. There is one reference that on one occasion a Moroccan ruler who had been forced out of power traveled to Mali (Holt, 1970, vol. 2). Needless to say, the long distances involved and the harsh terrain to cross must have served as deterrents of reciprocity.

It must be emphasized that these royal visits, although one-sided, reflected another dimension in which Islam provided the primary rationale and motive for these visits. Thus, as in the case of trade and scholarship, the religious dimension of Islam served as a major catalyst for the development of the Western Sudan's connections with the outside world. These royal visits to Egypt and Arabia were to serve the Western Sudan very well, for they not only spread the fame of the Western Sudanese rulers but also led to the increased level of interest on the part of numerous Islamic historians, who in turn left the only detailed written accounts about some of these rulers. Thus these royal visits proved historical not only for the visits *per se,* but also because of the influence they had on the development of the historiography of the Western Sudan.

The earliest recorded instance of a diplomatic note from a Western Sudanese ruler to the sovereign of another kingdom is the very brief reference in Al-Nazir's (twelfth century) writing. The author stated that he had come across a letter from a king of Ghana to the Yusuf b. Tashfin, a major leader of a region of Morocco. However, the author does not provide any more detail about the content of the letter.

In the fourteenth century during the time of Mansa Musa and his successor, there were more extensive diplomatic exchanges between ancient Mali and the Maghrib (Northwest Africa). Ibn Khaldun provides a few interesting details. He stated that diplomatic ties existed between the rulers of Mali and Sultan Abu 'l-Hasan, the king of the Maghrib, involving exchanges of envoys as well as gifts. According to Ibn Khaldun, both of the kingdoms designated high-ranking officials of their kingdoms as ambassadors and selected gifts for exchanges with much care (Levtzion & Hopkins, 1981). However, the author does not describe these gifts except that once a successor of Mansa Musa, Mari Jata, sent a giraffe all the way across the desert as his gift. The people of Morocco remembered this gift for a long time.

Mansa Musa is reported by Ibn Khladun to have sent a delegation in 1337 to the court of Sultan Hasan of the Maghrib to congratulate him on some of his conquests. The Malian delegation included a Sanhaja Berber as an interpreter. According to Ibn Khaldun, Abu 'l-Hasan "received them with honor, lodged them well, and sent them away fittingly. Desirous of displaying his customary opulence, he chose, from his household treasury, the rarest and most magnificent objects of Maghribi manufacture and appointed several of his courtiers...to convey them to the king of Mali" (Levtzion & Hopkins, 1981). The Sultan's delegation reached Mali after "much effort and long privation" and accomplished their mission. They, in turn, were well received and honored by the king of Mali who at the time was Mansa Sulayman, the brother and successor of Mansa Musa.

These diplomatic exchanges between Mali and the Maghrib continued over the next two decades. In 1348 Mali sent another mission to congratulate the Sultan for his conquest of Ifriqiya (Tunisia) and another one in the early 1360s. This latter one is described by Ibn Khaldun as follows: "The day of their arrival (in Fez) was a memorable one. The sultan (of Maghrib) sat to receive them in the Golden Tower as he would for a review and criers summoned the people to go out to the open space outside the city. They came out...until the space was too small for them and they climbed upon each other in the press round the giraffe in amazement at its form. The poets recited poems of eulogy and congratulation and description of the scene" (Levtzion & Hopkins, 1981). The Malian delegation greeted the sultan by spreading dust on their heads as was their custom and conveyed to the sultan the message of affection and friendship from their king.

Sultan Abu 'l-Hasan died in the early 1350s when Ibn Battuta was traveling through ancient Mali. Thus, he informs us that he attended a banquet held in honor of the deceased Moroccan sultan which was attended by important dignitaries of Mali and at which prayers were recited.

Unfortunately the early records do not inform us of the nature of diplomatic dialogues that occurred between these kingdoms or the consequences that emanated from them.

The earliest instances when the West African Muslim rulers sent their ambassadors to reside in the kingdoms with which they maintained diplomatic relations occurred in the late seventeenth century (Smith, 1973). These involved the relations between the kingdom of Bornu and the Ottoman empire and Morocco. Otherwise, the general pattern that can be discerned from the very limited sources is that during the period of ancient Mali the practice of posting a permanent envoy at the court of a foreign sovereign had not evolved. Diplomacy seemed to have been practiced in a very limited sense despite the fact that ancient Mali became the most famous African kingdom in its time, for Mali and Mansa Musa were recognized even by the European map makers of the 1330s and 1370s.

This chapter has shown that the economic, intellectual and diplomatic relations of ancient Mali were closely linked with the Islamic world. Islam had left an indelible mark on the history of the Western Sudan along with other parts of the African continent.

The impact of Islam upon the Western Sudan had been manifold. It integrated the Western Sudan into a universal cultural system. Islam greatly facilitated the preservation of the history of the region through the introduction and spread of the literate culture and the inclusion of anecdotes and descriptions about the Western Sudanese kingdoms in the chronicles written by many Muslim authors. Our debt to these chroniclers, as should be apparent from the material presented up to now, is immense. Islam introduced a new level of material culture in the Western Sudan which supplemented the region's economic growth.

However, Islam also had some negative effects upon the region. Most significant of these were cultural and demographic. The Islamic culture transplanted or superseded in many ways the traditional cultural practices of the peoples of the Western Sudan. From time to time, the Islamic religion served as an excuse for the waging of wars and conflicts (*jihads*) starting from the time of the Almoravids in the eleventh century to the nineteenth century Fulani *jihads*. In the demographic context, the most negative consequence of Islamic civilization upon the peoples of the Western Sudan was the development and/or the expansion in the slave trade that accompanied the Islamization of North Africa and lands to the south. The topic of slave trade and the Islamic world's involvement in it is discussed in detail in a later chapter. Suffice it to state here that the slave trade aspect of Islam's connection with the Western Sudan has often overshadowed, especially in the western world, some of the significant positive and beneficial consequences of the Western Sudan's links with the Islamic world. Mansa Musa and ancient Mali during his reign represent a most remarkable illustration of the Western Sudan's links with the Islamic world that resulted in the widespread recognition of this African empire as a major participant on the stage of world history and which left a lasting historical legacy.

CHAPTER IV

MANSA MUSA: THE GOLDEN KING

Introduction

As pointed out earlier, Sundiata Keita is regarded as the great founder of the empire of ancient Mali following the Battle of Krina around 1235. After waging a war to liberate his native state of Kangaba from the domination of the Soso people, Sundiata transformed the small state of Kangaba into the powerful empire of Mali. Sundiata's reign was followed, over the next fifty-five years, by seven other *Mansas* (kings) prior to the accession to power of Mansa Musa. These seven kings were Uli, Wati, Khalifa, Abu Bakr, Sakura, Qu and Muhammed. Mansa Uli, the son and immediate successor of Sundiata, is said to have been one of the most important kings. He continued the policy of conquest and expansion. Territories located in the present day countries of Senegal and Gambia are said to have been brought under the rule of Mali by Mansa Uli. Mansa Uli was succeeded by two brothers, Wati and Khalifa. These two brothers ruled for very short periods of four years and one year respectively. Mansa Khalifa is said to have suffered from some mental disorder. The next king, Abu Bakr, was a nephew of Sundiata. Mansa Abu Bakr's reign is said to have been marked by instability and dynastic conflicts. Following Abu Bakr's death, the Keita dynasty of kings established by Sundiata was temporarily interrupted. Sakura, a former slave, gained control of the throne. The exact circumstances that led to this shift of power in the uppermost echelon of ancient Mali's ruling class are not known. However, Sakura's reign is described as a successful one. Stability returned to the empire and numerous major conquests were undertaken. Mali's power and authority were widely acknowledged and trade flourished. Mansa Sakura died at the hands of robbers who murdered him in the Sahara Desert while he was returning from Mecca. After Sakura's death, succession was restored to the Sundiata Keita line. Mansa Qu, a great grandson of Sundiata, became the next ruler and he in turn was succeeded by his son, Mansa Muhammed.

Thus, by the time Mansa Musa came to the throne, the empire of Mali was well established. It had become the most important and dominant political entity in the Western Sudan by the early fourteenth century with important links with Islamic North Africa. Mansa Musa advanced the fame, power and prosperity of ancient Mali to its furthest extent. This chapter will summarize and synthesize what is described in the early Arabic accounts and the analyses of modern scholars regarding the life and times of Mansa Musa.

Accession to the Throne

The fourteenth century Arab writers Al-Umari (1301-1349) and Ibn Khaldun (1332-1406) have left us the most detailed contemporaneous accounts about Mansa Musa. These two writers, although neither one of them visited ancient Mali, have left more detailed accounts about Mansa Musa than Ibn Battuta who visited ancient Mali during the 1350s. Al Umari obtained his information about Mansa Musa and ancient Mali from several individuals who had either lived in Mali or had met and interacted with Mansa Musa during the latter's stay in Cairo in the 1320s. Al-Umari identifies the following as among his principal sources of information on Mansa Musa and ancient Mali: Abu Uthman Said al-Dukkali, who had lived in the capital city of Mali for thirty five-years and was a person who Al-Umari considered to be honest and reliable; Abu l' Hasan ali b. Amin Amir Hajib, an official at the court of the Sultan of Cairo who had met Mansa Musa and had held conversations with the ruler of Mali; Abu l'Ruh Isa al-Zawawi, a learned Egyptian theologian who had also met Mansa Musa and had held conversations with him; and numerous merchants of Cairo who had profited from Mansa Musa's entourage during their stay in the Egyptian city in the 1320s (Levtzion & Hopkins, 1981).

Ibn Khaldun identified the following individuals from whom he gathered valuable information about Mansa Musa and ancient Mali: Sheikh Uthman, a prominent and a highly learned theologian from the Western Sudan whom Ibn Khaldun had met in Egypt in 1394; Al-Muammar, a Northwest African political leader who had met Mansa Musa in order to enlist the Mansa's help in his struggle to gain power; Al-Hajj Yunus, a Malian interpreter who lived in Cairo; and Abu Abd Allah Muhammad b. Wasul, a Muslim judge who had settled in Kawkaw in the eastern region of ancient Mali (Levtzion & Hopkins, 1981). These informants provided brief but significant details about political, economic, religious and social conditions that existed in ancient Mali during the fourteenth century.

Mansa Musa himself is said to have provided an account describing the circumstances which resulted in his succeeding to the throne of Mali. This account was given by Mansa Musa to Ibn Amir Hajib, who in turn narrated it to Al-Umari. Ibn Amir Hajib was the governor of Old Cairo during Mansa Musa's visit to that city. The two men became friends and, according to Ibn Amir Hajib, the king of Mali shared a good deal of information about himself, his kingdom and its people.

Ibn Amir Hajib asked Mansa Musa how he came to be the ruler of Mali. Mansa Musa is said to have replied that he inherited the kingdom when his predecessor left on a long-distance voyage across the ocean. His predecessor, Mansa Muhammed, was intrigued by what lay beyond the Atlantic Ocean. According to this story, Mansa Muhammad's curiosity about what lay beyond the Atlantic Ocean was so great that he ordered 200 ships equipped with men, gold, water and supplies, and commanded the men not to return until they reached the end of the ocean or until they ran out of their supplies. The expedition departed and after a long time one ship returned. The captain of that ship reported to the Mansa that the expedition had traveled on the ocean for a long time until all the ships, except his, entered a powerful current in the ocean which carried them away. None of the ships could return and it was not known what happened to them. The captain added that he kept his ship out of the current and, therefore, was able to return to report to the king. Then the Mansa, out of disbelief, ordered two thousand more ships to be readied with men and supplies for a second expedition that he himself led. As Mansa Muhammed embarked on this large-scale expedition, he designated Mansa Musa to be in charge of the kingdom. Mansa Muhammad and those who accompanied him never returned and that is how Mansa Musa became the next ruler. This is how Mansa Musa himself explained his accession to the throne of ancient Mali (Levtzion & Hopkins, 1981).

The above account has given rise to important historical questions and controversy, such as the possibility of West Africans having crossed the Atlantic Ocean before Christopher Columbus; the technical and navigational skills of West Africans needed to travel on a vast body of water; and the possibility of African presence in the Americas before the beginning of the trans-Atlantic slave trade. These and related issues are the focus of the efforts of several modern scholars who are seeking to find answers to this "legend" of ancient Mali.

In the above story Mansa Musa did not clarify what his relationship was to his predecessor. Levtzion has suggested that the predecessor was not Mansa Musa's father. According to Levtzion, Mansa Musa's accession to the throne of Mali represented a departure in the line of succession. Mansa Musa was the son (according to some historians) or a grandson (according to Levtzion) of Abu Bakr, who was the brother of Sundiata, the founder of the empire of Mali. Thus, while the rulers of Mali prior to Mansa Musa were the sons and grandsons of Sundiata (except for Sakura, who is said to have been a former slave), the rulers from the time of Mansa Musa came from the family of Sundiata's brother. Some historians assert that Mansa Musa was born to Sundiata's sister (Trimingham, 1970). But Levtzion argues that this has been based on an erroneous translation of the Arabic text of Ibn Khaldun's account. In any event, this shift in the line of succession, that is from Sundiata's descendants to his brother's descendants, later on contributed to dynastic disputes and conflicts which significantly weakened the power of ancient Mali.

Mansa Musa ascended to the throne of Mali in 1312. He ruled for a quarter of a century until 1337. During his reign ancient Mali reached the peak of its power and fame. Sundiata Keita and Mansa Musa stand out as the two most prominent rulers of ancient Mali.

Mansa Musa's Reign

The fourteenth century Arabic sources provide us with some insights and information regarding the personality of Mansa Musa; the power of the Mansa within his realm and in the region; the royal manners and etiquette; and the nature of the governmental administration. Of all the kings of ancient Mali, Mansa Musa and his brother Mansa Sulayman, who ruled ancient Mali from 1341 to 1360, are the ones who are most often mentioned and described in the fourteenth century sources. Mansa Sulayman was the ruler during Ibn Battuta's visit to Mali. Following their rule, the empire entered the period of its decline. Among the factors that contributed to Mansa Musa's fame were the numerous conquests that had been undertaken which considerably extended the size of the empire of Mali; the wealth and generosity that was displayed by Mansa Musa; the expansion of Islamization that occurred in Mali in particular but the region as a whole; the royal pilgrimage to Mecca; the diplomatic contacts that took place between Mali and Morocco; and the availability of firsthand and eyewitness accounts and descriptions of life in ancient Mali during and shortly after the reign of Mansa Musa. These factors are explored in some detail below. The subject of the royal pilgrimage to Mecca is discussed in more detail in a later chapter.

Conquests

The territorial size of the empire was one important reason for the widespread fame of the rulers of ancient Mali in the fourteenth century. Mansa Musa expanded the domain of ancient Mali to its greatest extent. The earlier rulers of Mali, most notably Sundiata (c.1235-55), Mansa Uli (1255-70), and Sakura (1285-1300), had undertaken significant conquests that had established the foundation of imperial Mali. But during Mansa Musa's time, the empire was extended from the Atlantic coast to the east of the great bend of the Niger River (see map on page 20). Al-Umari listed the different territories that formed parts of the empire of Mali. Included in his list were Ghana, Zafun, Tirafka, Takrur, Sanghana, Banb'w, Zarqatabana, Damura, Zagha, Kabura, Bawaghuri, and Kawkaw (Levtzion & Hopkins, 1981). According to Al-Umari, altogether there were fourteen of these provinces that were under the domination and rule of Mali. Mansa Musa had mentioned to one of his hosts in Cairo that he and his army had conquered twenty-four cities and their surrounding territories. Most of the empire was populated. One of Al-Umari's sources indicated that it required four months' journey to cross the empire of Mali from north to south or from east to west. Of all the conquered territories only the ruler of Ghana, other than the Mansa of Mali, was permitted by the Mansa of Mali to use the title of the king.

Building up such a large empire naturally required a powerful military force. Al-Umari provides us some information regarding the military prowess of ancient Mali. He mentions that the ruler of Mali possessed the largest army in the Sudan and one which was the most successful against its enemies. The size of the army of Mali was estimated at 100,000 by Al-Umari with 10,000 of the troops mounted on horses. The Mansa imported horses from the Arabs at high costs. Those mounted soldiers who were recognized for their bravery wore golden bracelets and were rewarded with wide trousers which symbolized a prestigious status. No one, however, was allowed to wear trousers that were wider than those of the king.

The early sources also provide us some details about the weapons used by the army of ancient Mali. Al-Umari and Ibn Battuta, who during his stay in the capital of Mali in the 1350s witnessed Mansa Sulayman accompanied in the public ceremonies by his guards and soldiers, describe some of the weapons used by the Malian soldiers. These consisted mainly of lances, bows, arrows, quivers, spears, maces and swords. Some of these weapons described by Ibn Battuta were made of gold and silver and most probably were used for ceremonial purposes. An indication of the regional power of the Mansa of Mali is provided by Ibn Khaldun, who mentioned the case of Al-Mu'ammar, a descendent of a Moroccan ruler, who sought Mansa Musa's military assistance in a conflict with another ruler. Mansa Musa promised him assistance but no more is mentioned about the case.

As can be expected in a large-scale political kingdom, the military of ancient Mali was organized in an hierarchical order. Under the command of the Mansa were two principal generals known as Sangar-Zouma and Faran Souma—one for the northern region and the other for the southern region (Tall, 1977). Under each of these generals were additional levels of authorities. It was the responsibility of these officers to furnish and prepare the army. Troops were also contributed by the conquered tributary states.

One of the most important territories that formed a part of the empire of Mali was the region of Timbuktu. There exist conflicting accounts as to when and under which Mansa the city of Timbuktu was conquered. Some accounts give Mansa Musa the credit for having conquered it while others mention its conquest prior to Mansa Musa. However, Mansa Musa paid greater attention to Timbuktu and is said to have undertaken initiatives that contributed to the rise of Timbuktu as an economic, educational, political, and religious center in later years. Mansa Musa commissioned the construction of a major mosque in the city which stands to the present day (more detail about the mosque follows). Mansa Musa also ensured the loyalty of the cities of Gao and Jenne which had proved rebellious from time to time.

Royal Etiquette

Some interesting observations are recorded in the early sources regarding how the Mansas of Mali presented themselves in public and how the general populace was expected to behave towards the Malian rulers. As pointed out above, one rule mentioned by Al-Umari was that no man was allowed to wear trousers that were wider than those of the Mansa. Also, according to Al-Umari, sneezing in the presence of the Mansa was another taboo. A person who sneezed while the Mansa was in court was punished by a severe beating. On the other hand, if the Mansa sneezed, his attendees responded by beating on their chests. Persons who entered the Mansa's living quarters were required to remove their shoes. Failure to remove shoes either inadvertently or on purpose, according to Al-Umari, resulted in a death penalty. When a person was granted an audience with the ruler, the custom was for the person to sprinkle ashes on his own head as a sign of respect to the sovereign. Another royal custom was that the Mansa did not eat in the presence of anybody. Even when Mansa Musa was in Cairo, he is said to have always eaten alone. And, as Ibn Battuta described, the Mansa always communicated with his visitors through an interpreter. We learn from Ibn Battuta that this custom of the ruler communicating with his subjects through an interpreter was also practiced by regional and provincial administrators. Ibn Battuta observed this practice in Walata, his own first major stop in ancient Mali. He described the visit of a group of merchants to the local Malian administrator (*farba*) who addressed the visitors through an interpreter. Ibn Battuta regarded this practice as a sign of contempt towards the visitors. Ibn Amir Hajib, the Egyptian official and governor of Old Cairo, recounted that when he visited Mansa Musa upon the latter's arrival in Cairo to welcome him to Egypt on behalf of the Egyptian Sultan, the Malian ruler showed him great courtesy but spoke to him only through an interpreter although Mansa Musa was said to be quite fluent in the Arabic language. It must be noted that this is a custom that is being practiced even in the present time in a number of West African cultures in which a key member of the ruler's staff is the linguist who serves as the communications link between the king and his subjects.

Another interesting episode that serves to illustrate the etiquette among the Mansas of Mali is recorded by Al-Umari based upon information provided by Abu l' Abbas al-Haq, an Egyptian official. When Mansa Musa arrived in Cairo in 1324, he initially refused to pay a visit to the Sultan of Egypt. The Mansa's excuse was that he was on his way to Mecca to perform the pilgrimage and did not wish to mix any other activity to distract him from his main goal. The Egyptian protocol, on the other hand, required that the Mansa pay a courtesy visit to the Egyptian sovereign. After a great deal of persistence on the part of the Egyptian official, Al-Haq, Mansa Musa agreed to visit the Sultan. Al-Haq explained that the reason Mansa Musa did not want to visit the Sultan was that he did not want to prostrate or bow before the Egyptian sovereign as was the custom. When Mansa Musa arrived for his visit with the Sultan and was asked to prostrate and kiss the ground, he refused. A crisis in diplomatic protocol was averted, however, when an advisor of Mansa Musa whispered some advice to him. Mansa Musa prostrated but stated that he was prostrating to God who had created him. Mansa Musa, a sovereign who himself was used to having people prostrate before him, must have regarded the act of prostration as more than just a symbol of diplomatic protocol, perhaps a sign of subservience. Fisher (1970) has suggested that Mansa Musa may have exempted some foreign visitors to his court from prostrating on racial grounds. Fisher may be suggesting that some lighter-skinned Muslim or non-Muslim visitors to the court of Mansa Musa were probably granted such exemptions. Such an assertion, however, begs for some evidentiary indication which Fisher does not identify. In any case, following this incident, the two sovereigns of Mali and Egypt went on to converse for a long time. The Sultan of Egypt presented the Malian ruler and his entourage with numerous gifts that included robes, horses, swords, skull-caps, belts and other items some of which were made in gold. Mansa Musa had presented to the Egyptian court quantities of Malian gold and other valuables.

Both Ibn Battuta and Al-Umari have provided some descriptions of the court of the Mansa of Mali, especially on public occasions. On such occasions, the Mansa sat on a large ebony throne placed on a platform, which was decorated all around with many elephant tusks. The Mansa was surrounded by guards, slaves, flag-bearers, parasol carriers and principal political and military officials. Many public performers—musicians, singers, dancers and poets—must have made such gatherings colorful and entertaining. At such functions, the Mansa usually dressed in tunics, wide trousers, turbans and gold jewelry. Al-Bakri recorded similar descriptions regarding the public assemblies held by the kings of ancient Ghana in the eleventh century. The ordinary subjects of the Mansas displayed great submissiveness towards the sovereign. Ibn Battuta regarded the Western Sudanese as the most submissive of all the people that he encountered.

Wealth

Mansa Musa's widespread fame was partly due to the wealth that was supposed to have been at his disposal. The fourteenth century rulers of Mali were reputed to be the richest ones in the Western Sudan. This reputation was not based on idle rumors. The cornerstone of the wealth of ancient Mali was gold. The gold fields of Bambuk and Bure yielded thousands of ounces of the precious metal over several centuries. It was the lure of the gold that led so many traders to risk the dangers of crossing the Sahara Desert. Besides the traders who helped spread the fame of Mali as a land of wealth, it was the Mansas of Mali, through their use and display of gold, who contributed to this image. And among the Mansas of ancient Mali, it was none other than Mansa Musa whose lavish use of gold singularly resulted in the acknowledgment of ancient Mali as the richest black African kingdom. The rulers of Mali received great quantities of gold in the form of tribute. They, in turn, used the gold to reward prominent chiefs and officials of the kingdom and to pay for expenses. Al-Umari recorded that some of these officials received as much as 50,000 *mithqals* (1 mithqal equaled about one-eighth ounce) of gold from the Mansa per year. However, it was the amount gold that was taken by Mansa Musa on his pilgrimage that contributed to the reputation of ancient Mali as the richest land in Black Africa. Early accounts inform us that Mansa Musa had taken with him eighty to one hundred loads of gold weighing about two thousand pounds. Mansa Musa spent some of this gold for his expenses and gave away a good amount of it in charity and gifts. Again, contemporary witnesses have left some amazing accounts of Mansa Musa's generosity. According to one of Al-Umari's informants, Mansa Musa flooded Cairo with his generosity. No *emir* or royal official in the court of the ruler of Egypt was left without receiving a gift of gold from Mansa Musa. And the merchants of Cairo earned large sums of gold from the entourage of Mansa Musa who shopped in the bazaars of Cairo. Al-Umari recorded that gold had enjoyed a high price (25 *dirhams*) in Egypt until the arrival of Mansa Musa. After the visit of Mansa Musa, the price of gold fell down to 22 *dirhams* and remained low for twelve years due to the large quantity of gold that was spent in Egypt by Mansa Musa and his entourage. In fact, Mansa Musa spent all his wealth before completing his journey. When he returned to Cairo from Mecca for his homeward journey, he was forced to take a loan from wealthy Egyptian merchants. Ibn Battuta would also certainly have appreciated Mansa Musa's generosity. In fact, one of the very few observations that Ibn Battuta made about Mansa Musa in his narrative is that Mansa Musa was a generous and a virtuous ruler.

Besides gold, copper was another mineral that added to the wealth of ancient Mali. Mansa Musa stated to one of the native Arabs of the Hijaz with whom he became acquainted that copper was the only commodity that was taxed and it was traded for gold. Ibn Battuta visited the copper-producing region of Taggada in the 1350s but at that time this region was independent and not under the control of Mali. Finally, salt was the third major mineral that played a key part in the economy of ancient Mali.

While it was the international trade of Mali and its wealth in gold that gave it such widespread fame, the majority of the people of ancient Mali lived in rural areas and were subsistence farmers. For them the agricultural sector of the kingdom's economy was much more important. The early sources, again, are quite helpful in providing us some insights into this aspect of ancient Mali. Ibn Battuta, during his travels through Mali, noted that the following agricultural products were in wide use: millet, rice, beans and a grain that resembled mustard seed. Milk, honey, certain fruits and chickens are other products frequently mentioned. Al-Umari informs us that the means of subsistence in ancient Mali was meager and selection of food items were few although the kingdom was quite verdant. Wheat was quite scarce. Turnips, cowpeas, onions, garlic, cabbage, aubergines, gourds and some varieties of root crops are among the other products that are mentioned by Al-Umari that were under cultivation in Mali. The kingdom is reported to have been rich in livestock, mostly consisting of cattle, sheep and goats.

Islamization

During the reign of Mansa Musa, especially after his return from Mecca, the influence of Islam is believed to have spread more extensively in Mali. Mansa Musa himself is described in the fourteenth century sources as a pious and religious ruler. Ibn Amir

Hajib, the Egyptian official who met Mansa Musa, described him to be quite attentive to his prayer obligations and the reading of the Quran.

Although Islam is said to have been accepted by the Mansas of Mali for decades before the time of Mansa Musa, it is Mansa Musa who is given credit for instituting certain practices that are central to Islamic culture. Al-Umari implies that it was Mansa Musa who ordained the Friday prayers, the use of the *muezzin* (the prayer caller), and the congregational prayers. It is not clear why these basic elements of Islam had not taken root earlier. Another interesting anecdote mentioned in Al-Umari's account about Mansa Musa and Islam is that Mansa Musa became aware for the first time while he was in Cairo that a Muslim man, including a king, is not allowed to have more than four wives. According to Malian custom, the king commonly received beautiful women as gifts from his subjects. When informed that this was incompatible with Islamic law, Mansa Musa pleaded ignorance of the law and committed to end the practice. It is not known whether he followed through with this commitment.

One of the lasting legacies of Mansa Musa's pro-Islamic policies was the construction of numerous mosques in his kingdom, most notably the mosque in Timbuktu. This mosque, which underwent renovations a few times over the centuries, stands to the present day as a vital link with the past. This is the *Jingerebir* mosque, one of the three renowned ancient mosques built in Timbuktu. It is said that while Mansa Musa was in Arabia during his pilgrimage, he met a Muslim poet and architect who was from Granada in Spain. Mansa Musa expressed his interest in having the architect come to Mali, and the architect, Abu Ishaq Ibrahim al-Sahili, warmly accepted the invitation and accompanied Mansa Musa to Mali on his return journey. Mansa Musa is said to have commissioned Al-Sahili to undertake the construction of mosques in Gao and Timbuktu and a royal palace in the capital. It was a common practice among Islamic rulers to commission the construction of mosques. It enhanced their prestige as well as demonstrated their commitment to the faith. Ibn Khaldun recorded that Mansa Musa was pleased with Al-Sahili's work on a royal residential building and that he paid him 12,000 *mithqals* (about 1,500 ounces) of gold dust. Al-Sahili lived for the rest of his life in Mali. He died and was buried in Timbuktu. Ibn Battuta, during his brief stay in Timbuktu, visited the famous architect's grave.

The *Jingerebir* mosque became the principal mosque in Timbuktu and has remained so for most of the history of that city.

As the principal mosque it served as the chief venue for the Friday congregational prayer. During the height of the Malian power, it is believed that the major scholars and dignitaries from all over Timbuktu gathered at this mosque for the Friday and festival prayer observances (Saad, 1983). The *imams* (principal religious leaders) of the *Jingerebir* mosque were acknowledged as among the most important local leaders. Many distinguished and learned individuals served as the *imams* of this mosque. Saad (1983) has compiled a fascinating list of some of these *imams* of the *Jingerebir* mosque from the fourteenth century to the early twentieth century. Rene Caillie, the famous French explorer who visited Timbuktu in the 1820s, spent much time at the *Jingerebir* mosque observing the life of the city and recording his notes from atop the minaret. He commented upon the ruined condition of parts of the mosque. Caillie observed that the newer parts of the mosque were quite inferior in comparison to the ancient ones. Heinrich Barth, during his visit to the city in the 1850s, was quite impressed by the large size and the "stately appearance" of the mosque. Barth, as a non-Muslim, was not allowed to enter the mosque, so he could only explore the mosque from the outside. During the supremacy of the Songhay empire in the sixteenth century, the Sankore mosque had become more important and famous as the gathering place of the city's literati.

Thus, Mansa Musa is recognized as one of the two principal rulers of ancient Mali in the fourteenth century to have greatly advanced the presence and influence of Islam in the kingdom. According to Hrbek and El Fasi (1992), "The Islamic outlook of the empire took shape in the fourteenth century under Mansa Musa and his brother Mansa Sulayman, who encouraged the building of mosques and the development of Islamic learning."

Law and Justice

Ibn Battuta made a very complimentary observation about the people of Mali. He stated that among the admirable qualities possessed by the black people of Mali was that they were rarely unjust. He observed that no other people had a greater dislike for injustice than the people of Mali. This is quite a praiseworthy observation considering that Ibn Battuta had visited so many other lands in the Middle East, Asia and Africa before his visit to Mali. He further observed that one could travel through the kingdom of Mali with a great sense of safety and security. Strangers or the local inhabitants had no cause to fear for their safety from robbers or men of violence.

However, existence of a variety of crimes is attested to in some of the early records. Even Ibn Battuta mentioned that when he and the group of the trans-Saharan caravan merchants first arrived in the northern Malian town Walata, they did not feel safe in leaving their merchandise unattended. Mansa Musa also alluded to the existence of the crime of theft, particularly in reference to gold. During his stay in Egypt, Mansa Musa is said to have acknowledged in his conversations with the Egyptian hosts that some theft of gold was a matter of fact in his kingdom, and that his own wealth in gold was diminished by what people stole.

The legal system that was practiced in ancient Mali was a two-track system—traditional and Islamic. A majority of the people of ancient Mali, especially in the rural areas, were not Muslims until much later centuries. They, therefore, relied on their traditional and customary norms to seek redress or punishment for transgressions. In major towns and trading centers, a larger segment of the population was often Muslim and, therefore, the *shariah* (Islamic law) supposedly constituted the foundation and provided the framework for the administration of their legal system.

In the application of both of these types of judicial frameworks—traditional or Islamic—the Mansa, as can be expected, played a central part. In the functioning of the traditional system of justice, the Mansa himself was regarded and served as the final judge. He personally became involved in receiving complaints, hearing cases, and rendering judgments. This was his prerogative. The people, at least in the capital cities, had access and opportunities to present their grievances at the highest level. Although Ibn Battuta informs us that ancient Mali offered a great deal of safety and security to natives and foreigners alike, the kingdom was not quite crime-free.

According to Al-Umari's account, one of the most common types of crime that was committed in ancient Mali was the practice of sorcery, the use or perceived use of supernatural power with evil intentions to bring harm to another human being. Sorcery was and in many cultures is, up to the present time, regarded as a real phenomenon which is capable of causing misfortune, illness, and even death to an enemy or to an offending party. Al-Umari, based upon his informant Al-Dukkali, who had lived in Mali for thirty five years, recorded that the Mansa of Mali heard and passed judgment upon a vast number of cases involving the practice of sorcery and, if the accused were found guilty, they were put to death. It will be recalled here that in the history of the rise of ancient Mali, the evil powers of sorcery were closely associated with Sumanguru, the tyrant and the oppressor of the pre-empire Mali. The early records also inform us that capital punishment was used in convictions involving crimes of theft. Al-Umari informs us that the Mansa also heard grievances and complaints from his subjects about bureaucratic excesses, although no specific examples or cases are recorded. Thus, in the administration of justice based upon the traditional jurisprudence, the Mansa was the final and absolute judge. His word was often the law and his verdict was the last word.

In addition to the Mansa judgment, the Islamic judicial tradition was the second legal system that came to be practiced in ancient Mali and in other parts of the Western Sudan where Islam had taken root. As pointed out earlier, *Sunni* Islam was the branch that became dominant in the Western Sudan. The Islamic judicial system did not grant the Mansa of Mali the absolute power as did the traditional system. In fact, some accounts suggest that there were towns in ancient Mali where the Mansa exercised no judicial authority. In the Islamic tradition, the *qadi* (judge) played the major part in the administration of law which essentially involved the interpretation and application of *shariah* (the Quranic law). In situations where there were Muslim communities that lived in states ruled by non-Muslim rulers, such as ancient Ghana, records inform us that the rulers allowed the Muslims the privilege of autonomy in working out their own system according to Islamic law. But, as more and more Western Sudanese rulers became converted to Islam, these rulers themselves became more involved in exercising influence and control over the system.

The interpretation and the application of Islamic law, by necessity, had to be delegated to individuals who were very learned and well versed in the Quran and the traditions of the Prophet Muhammad. The *qadis* (Muslim judges) were normally selected or appointed from among this group of learned individuals. In cases where the kings and the rulers were Muslims, as was the case in ancient Mali in the fourteenth century, the rulers appointed the *qadis* of various towns. Thus, this was the scenario in ancient Mali during Mansa Musa's reign. He exercised the power of appointing the *qadis*. However, it must also be emphasized that the *qadis* were most frequently paid and maintained through the state treasury. Thus, this was another way in which the rulers influenced the administration of justice.

A very important manner in which the ruler of the state could and did influence the administration of the Islamic judicial pattern was through favoring one school of law over others. As pointed out earlier, in Islam there are four major schools of jurisprudence within the *Sunni* branch—the Hanafi, Maliki, Shafii and Hanbali. A detailed discussion of the differences among these schools is beyond the scope of this work. However, Mansa Musa is said to have favored the Maliki school. This school was founded in the eighth century in Medina by Malik ibn Anas. According to this school, the body of Islamic law consisted of, in addition to the Quran and the Hadiths, the consensus of the early community of Medina. Al-Umari informs us that upon Mansa Musa's return to Mali from Arabia and Egypt he brought along with him scholars of the Maliki school.

Ibn Battuta mentioned one interesting case which was narrated to him by a Malian official in the 1350s. This case involved a "white" (light-skinned Berber or Arab) *qadi*, who had accompanied Mansa Musa on his return from Egypt. This man is said to have attempted to steal about five hundred ounces of gold. Mansa Musa was greatly angered by this and punished him by exiling this man to the land of the pagan cannibals where he is said to have lived among them for four years after which the Mansa sent him back to his country of origin. According to ibn Battuta, this man's "whiteness" saved him because he was regarded as unripe by the alleged cannibals. Ibn Battuta also cites another episode which described Mansa Musa's generosity. In this episode, a Moroccan man had once given a gift to Mansa Musa when Musa was a young boy and had not yet become a ruler. Later, this same man appeared before Musa, who by then had become the Mansa, to settle a certain dispute. Mansa Musa recognized this man and invited him to come close to him. Then Mansa Musa gave this man a gift in gold one hundred times the amount of gift that the man had given him previously. In addition, the Mansa presented him with a robe and slaves (Levtzion & Hopkins, 1981). This story was narrated to Ibn Battuta by the son of the man who was an Islamic teacher in Mali and met Ibn Battuta during his travels through Mali.

Finally, one other way in which Mansa Musa is said to have enhanced Islamization in ancient Mali was through sending Malians to study in other Islamic countries, particularly in Fez, Morocco. One of the most prominent Malians to have been sent to Fez was Katib Musa, who became a leading *qadi* in Timbuktu in the fourteenth century (Saad, 1983).

Question of the Capital City

One of the mysteries associated with the history of ancient Mali, including Mansa Musa's period, concerns the name and location of the capital of the kingdom. The early written sources refer to the capital of ancient Mali by a variety of names but they do not use the name which is most commonly used by many of the modern scholars in their identification of the ancient capital. Hunwick (1973) and Tall (1977) have presented excellent summaries of the different points of view regarding this question. Ibn Battuta, who stayed in the capital of ancient Mali for several months, observed that a visitor needed to obtain permission before entering the capital of Mali which was located near a river. Was this reference to the Senegal River or a tributary of the Niger River? This is one of the unresolved issues. Secondly, Ibn Battuta used the name Mali to refer to the capital city as well as to the kingdom, thus adding to the confusion. The oral traditions give the name Niani to the capital. Al-Umari, based upon his informants, uses the name of Byty to refer to the capital of ancient Mali, and Ibn Khaldun refers to the capital by the name Bny. Modern archaeology, according to Niane (1984) and Tall, seems to support Niani as the capital which is located along a tributary of the Niger. However, this question is far from being conclusively resolved.

Apart from the issues of the name and location of the capital of ancient Mali, what did the early authors have to say about the capital of one of the most powerful and famous kingdoms of medieval Africa? Our major sources—Ibn Battuta, Al-Umari and Ibn Khaldun—provide very minimal information. Ibn Battuta, who spent eight months in the capital of Mali, observed that there was a separate residential quarter for the 'whites' where he himself stayed and that the *qadi* was black. He described the scenes of royal assemblies. He also described getting very sick while in the capital. Al-Umari described the town as extensive in size. While the town itself was not surrounded by a wall, he mentioned that the king had numerous palaces in the town that were enclosed by walls. The buildings were made of clay and the town was surrounded by rivers. Ibn Khaldun stated that the capital of Mali was a large place and well cultivated. It was densely populated and had busy markets. Trading caravans came there from Morocco, Tunisia and Egypt bearing goods from many lands.

The famous poet-architect Al-Saheli, whom Mansa Musa brought back with him from Arabia, is said to have built a beautiful reception salon in one of the Mansa's palaces in Niani. Since Al-Saheli was of Granadan origin, he is said to have designed this salon in the style of Spanish-Islamic architecture incorporating colorful arabesques. Mansa Musa was said to have been very pleased with the work and rewarded the architect very generously. Unfortunately, this work has not survived. According to Niane, "With the successive destructions of Niani and the wearing away of the plaster under years of rain, the poet-architect's great achievement was finally reduced to a heap of clay and rubble" (1984).

Political Organization

Ancient Mali was an imperial system made up of numerous conquered peoples and states. The population included various Sudanese groups, some Arabs, and a much larger number of Berbers of the Sahara. A vast majority of the people practiced traditional religions. Islam, as pointed out earlier, was the religion of the mainly urban-dwellers, traders, and members of the ruling class. Although the Mansa was the highest authority of the empire, the empire is said to have been a conglomeration of autonomous and semi-autonomous provinces rather than a tightly controlled centralized system. Besides the ruler of Mali, according to Al-Umari, only one other subject-sovereign was allowed to carry the title of the king, and that was the ruler of Ghana.

Again, Ibn Battuta has left us some clues regarding aspects of the political organization of ancient Mali. During his travels through different parts of Mali, he met with a variety of officials. In some places he encountered officials who represented the Mansa of Mali. This was the case in Walata, Timbuktu and a couple of other towns. These officials were known by the title of *farba* (deputy). One gets the impression that the *farba* was the highest official and the principal administrator of the town as well as the province. The *farba* held their own court assemblies that seemed to be patterned after the royal assemblies held by the Mansa in the capital city. Ibn Battuta, who described the great royal assemblies of Mansa Sulayman (1341-1360), also described the scene when the *farba* of Walata welcomed and received Ibn Battuta and his companion travelers when they arrived in this northernmost town of ancient Mali. The *farba*, dressed in the official regalia, was surrounded by his guards and other dignitaries bearing a variety of arms. And like the Mansa he also addressed the visitors through an interpreter. These *farba* of the towns appointed additional officials to administer smaller sections of the towns. These officials were provided with robes, turbans and trousers as symbols of their office. The kingdom of Mali was said to have had fourteen provinces at its peak. The provinces were further subdivided into villages administered by traditional chiefs accountable to the provincial administrator. The provincial administrators collected tributes, maintained law and order, and recruited soldiers for the army. Those who performed their duties well were generously rewarded in gold, horses and clothes by the Mansa. From time to time, the provincial administrators presented themselves at Mansa's court to give reports of their actions and provide details of revenue collections.

Ibn Battuta also mentioned the presence of another rank of official in the town of Walata. This rank was the *mushrif* (inspector). What exactly this inspector did or what his functions were is not detailed. Presumably he oversaw the imports and exports that passed through the town. Ibn Battuta cited the case of the *mushrif* of Walata who was accused of having swindled a Berber merchant. The merchant complained and pleaded for justice from Mansa Sulayman. The Mansa recalled the official from his post in Walata and referred the case to a *qadi*. The merchant was found in the right and was compensated while the official was terminated from his job (Levtzion & Hopkins, 1981). In the case of Mansa Musa, Al-Umari informs us that the Mansa himself heard complaints and grievances brought against state officials and pronounced judgments in such cases.

Numerous other officials who formed part of the kingdom's administrative structure are identified in some of the early sources. These included the *dugha*, the *viziers* and the *emirs*. These titles reflect the blending of the traditional offices and functions with those that were adapted from the Islamic political culture.

Al-Umari and Ibn Battuta both provide us with examples of provinces within the empire of Mali which were ruled by their own native ruling families but which acknowledged the suzerainty of the king of Mali. Ibn Battuta provides examples of provinces of Kabara and Zagha which were ruled by their own sultans who gave allegiance to the Mansa of Mali. Al-Umari cited the case of the Berber state of Yantasar. In general, the subject states and kingdoms that were regarded as more loyal to the imperial rule were allowed to keep their local ruling classes as long as they did not rebel and as long as they paid their tributes. An important practice in these arrangements was that some members of the royal family of the subject state were taken as 'captives' or 'hostages' to the court of the emperor. The Western Sudanese author As-Sadi mentioned that this custom was commonly practiced in ancient Mali. These royal hostages were not necessarily treated as prisoners. They were given important positions and assignments in the administration of the Mansa. This supposedly was a measure undertaken to ensure the loyalty of the subject state as well as to strengthen the bonds between the conqueror and the conquered. However, this practice did not always bear the expected fruits. One of the most famous examples of such royal hostages who were brought to live at the court of the Mansa of Mali was Sonni Ali-Kolon, a prince of Songhay, after the conquest of Songhay by Mali. Ali-Kolon eventually escaped from Mali in the late 1200s and successfully waged a war of liberation against Mali. Ali-Kolon's victory resulted in regaining of independence by Songhay and laid the foundation for the evolution of Songhay into a major imperial system in the fifteenth century. In the process Ali-Kolon replaced the old Dia or Ja dynasty and initiated a new dynasty, the Sonni. However, Mansa Musa reconquered Songhay for a few years in the fourteenth century.

Despite the fact that Mansa Musa and many of his officials were familiar with a literate culture and possessed the knowledge of writing in Arabic language, the Malian political culture was largely an oral one. Al-Umari, citing his informant Al-Dukkali, observed that in general nothing was written down in the court of the Mansa even though there were scribes.

Slaves are also said to have played important roles in the overall society of ancient Mali. They were crucial in the economic, military, administrative and political activities (Levtzion, 1976). The subject of slaves is discussed in more detail in a later chapter. Suffice it to state here that appointments of slaves to positions of political importance is said to have been a characteristic of the political culture of ancient Mali.

The military structure and organization of the state is what gave security and endurance to its political power. The military in ancient Mali was closely controlled by the Mansa. The Mansa himself assumed the title of the commander-in-chief. The Mansas maintained direct control over certain segments of the military. The Mansas themselves are said to have led their armies on the battlefields and conquests but specific details are lacking in the early sources. Under the Mansa were two generals appointed by him. During Mansa Musa's reign Saran Mandian was one of the generals who did much to spread Mali's domination in the region of the Sahel (Niane, 1984). Military contingents were stationed in principal towns such as Walata, Gao and others.

Ibn Battuta, in his description of the scene of the royal assembly of Mansa Sulayman (Mansa Musa's brother) in 1352, observed that after the Mansa had made his grand entrance onto the stage and had taken his seat, three slaves then ran out and summoned the Mansa's deputy and his military generals. The identity, role and function are not described nor is his blood relationship, if any, to the Mansa explained. Tall suggests that the custom of the Mansa having a deputy goes back to the time of Sundiata. According to some Malinke traditions, Sundiata had designated his own half-brother as his deputy. So, perhaps, this tradition had continued into the fourteenth century.

A discussion of the political culture and organization of ancient Mali would not be complete without the mention of the office of the *griot*. This was a hereditary office, and in the court of the Mansa the *griot* came from the Kouyate clan and was a descendent of Balla Fasseke, the *griot* of Sundiata (Niane, 1984). Along with numerous other functions, the *griot* served as the spokesman of the Mansa, a tutor of the princes, and was in charge of the court music.

To maintain the political organization of the empire of Mali, needless to state, required significant amounts of resources and revenues. These were derived through taxation on trade, tributes collected from subject states, maintaining a monopoly-type control over gold, especially the gold nuggets, and taxation on harvests and livestock.

Ancient Mali, during the reigns of Mansa Musa and Mansa Sulayman, maintained diplomatic relations with the sultans of Morocco. As detailed earlier, the early sources confirm that these diplomatic exchanges were regarded as important and involved ambassadorial visits by high-ranking officials of the two kingdoms. These exchanges demonstrate that the culture of international diplomacy was valued and appreciated.

Thus, Mali under Mansa Musa was a complex imperial system. Although diverse in its population make-up, his rule represented the apogee of the Malinke people of the Western Sudan. As-Sadi, the sixteenth century Timbuktu scholar and author of the *Tarikh as-Sudan* (Chronicle of the Sudan), described Mansa Musa as having no equals among the rulers of ancient Mali in piety and courage. Although Islam was a religion of only a minority, the fact that this minority was the ruling and aristocratic class of the empire gave Mali a prominent place in the world of Islam.

There is no doubt that Mali would have gained some fame in medieval times due to its production and export of gold. But it probably would not have received as detailed and widespread attention as it did had it not been for the famous pilgrimage that Mansa Musa undertook during the middle of his twenty-five year reign. Due to the great importance of this pilgrimage in spreading the fame about Mansa Musa and the empire of ancient Mali, this pilgrimage will be discussed in some detail in the next chapter.

CHAPTER V

THE PILGRIMAGE TO MECCA

Introduction

The performance of the *hajj* (pilgrimage) is one of the five principal obligations in Islam that the believers are expected to fulfill. A devout Muslim who has the financial means and physical ability is expected to perform the *hajj* at least once in his or her lifetime. This obligation is mentioned in several verses in the Quran that not only state this requirement but also provide detailed instructions regarding the timing and the rituals that must be followed and observed during the performance of the pilgrimage. There are two types of pilgrimages that are mentioned in the Quran—the *hajj*, the Great Pilgrimage, and the *umra*, the Little Pilgrimage (*The Encyclopedia of Islam*, vol. III, 1979). The differences between the two are explained below.

According to the Islamic beliefs, the performance of the pilgrimage was first commanded by Allah through Abraham, who is regarded as a major prophet in the Islamic tradition as he is in the Judeo-Christian tradition. The Muslim tradition also links Abraham with the establishment of the first house of worship—the House of Lord—in what became the city of Mecca. "Verily the first sanctuary appointed for mankind was that at Bakkah, a blessed place, a guidance to the people" (Quran, Sura 3: 96). It was to the area of Mecca, according to Islam, that Abraham had brought Hagar and their infant son Ishmael when she was forced away by Sarah. Some of the rituals performed during the *hajj* (described below) are associated with and recall the suffering experienced by Hagar and Ishmael in Mecca. The following two verses in the Quran (Sura 22:26,27) establish this linkage between Abraham and the pilgrimage:

> Behold! We gave the site, to Abraham, of the (Sacred) House (Saying): "Associate not anything (in worship) with Me; and sanctify My House For those who compass it round or stand up, or bow, or prostrate themselves (therein in prayer).

>And proclaim the Pilgrimage Among men: they will
>come to thee on foot and (mounted) on every kind
>of camel, lean on account of journeys through deep
>and distant mountain highways.

Thus, when Allah commanded the performance of the pilgrimage through Prophet Muhammad, Allah reinstituted an old tradition. Although the tradition of the pilgrimage is said to have continued during the intervening years between the time of Abraham down to the days before the birth of the Prophet Muhammad, the rituals are believed to have become more pagan rather than following the tradition of Abraham. The House of the Lord had been desecrated during the intervening years through the introduction of idols commemorating pagan gods. The holy sanctuary had become a pagan shrine. Thus, with the prophethood of Muhammad, Mecca was cleansed and purified and the tradition of pilgrimage in honor of Allah was once again restored. Though some of the rituals performed during the *hajj* are rituals that are said to have been practiced by the Arabs of Mecca in the days preceding the revelation of Islam to Muhammad.

The performance of the *hajj* is commanded in Sura (Chapter) 2, Ayat (Verse) 196 as follows: "And complete the *hajj* or *umra* in the service of God." In the fourteen hundred years since the death of the Prophet Muhammad in A.D. 632, the *hajj* has grown to become the largest religious gathering in the world. The principal *hajj* can only be performed during the time that is specified in the Quran. The *umra* or the Little Pilgrimage, on the other hand, may be performed at any time during the year. Nowadays, nearly two million faithful Muslims from all corners of the world converge on Mecca for the principal *hajj* during the specified month and days. The pilgrims are expected to follow fixed rituals that are prescribed in the Quran and the *hadith* (sayings) of the Prophet Muhammad. The Prophet himself performed the *hajj* about three months before his death in A.D. 632 and during this pilgrimage he set down instructions, in addition to those provided in the Quran, regarding the performance of the *hajj*.

Rites and Rituals

The Quran is quite specific in detailing the manner and conditions for the performance of the *hajj*. It lists several of the rituals and practices that must be followed and observed. The first major requirement focuses upon the timing. The principal rites of the pilgrimage must be undertaken and completed during the first ten days of the last month in the Islamic calendar. This is the month of *Dhul-Hijjah* (literally the month of the pilgrimage). One may begin the pilgrimage during the tenth month of the year, but the major rituals must be performed only during the month of *Dhul-Hijjah*. In Islam, before one commences the rituals associated with the fulfillment of principal obligations, one must declare intent. Thus declaration of intent to perform the pilgrimage is a most important step. Before embarking on the pilgrimage journey, the believer must declare his intent to Allah concerning the purpose of his or her journey. Furthermore, believers who undertake to perform the pilgrimage are commanded to refrain from acts of obscenity, wickedness and quarrelling. The pilgrims are reminded that the best provision to accompany them during their pilgrimage is right conduct.

One important requirement during the pilgrimage is that all the pilgrims must wear prescribed pilgrim's garments. All men must dress in two pieces of seamless white cotton cloth and simple sandals. While women may wear their normal but simple clothes, they must keep their faces and hands uncovered. Women do not wear the veil during the pilgrimage. Many pilgrims put on these garments even before they reach the Holy City. This custom of every pilgrim wearing similar and simple garments symbolizes the equality of all believers in the eyes of Allah irrespective of wealth, status, or race. Prophet Muhammad had established several points, ranging in distance from forty-five kilometers to about four hundred kilometers from Mecca, at which the pilgrims must change to wearing the prescribed attire. While donning the specified attire, the pilgrim must also declare his or her intention as to whether the journey constitutes a *hajj* or an *umra*. These days the pilgrims, especially those traveling by air, don the specified clothing at the start of their journey in their home countries or change to the pilgrim's attire at transit airports like Cairo. When the pilgrims put on these garments, they enter the state of *ihram* (prohibition) during which time the pilgrims are forbidden to clip nails, cut hair, hunt, use perfume or engage in sexual activity. These are regarded as acts of vanity and must be put aside during the duration of the pilgrimage. Also, no marriage proposals or contracts must be entertained or entered into during the pilgrimage. The pilgrims' focus henceforth must be on prayers and worship of Allah.

The city of Mecca, where the rites of the pilgrimage take place, is the epicenter of the Islamic world. It is regarded as so sacred by the Muslims that no non-Muslims are allowed to enter the Holy City. This restriction has been in place since the time of Prophet Muhammad when the city was conquered by Muslims, and pagans and non-believers were prohibited from entering the sacred precincts. Even airplanes carrying non-Muslims are forbidden to fly over the city. However, there have been instances when Christians have managed to visit Mecca under disguise. Prior to the nineteenth century only two European Christians are believed to have succeeded in visiting Mecca—Lodovico Bartema of Rome in 1603 and Joseph Pitts of England in 1680 (Burton, 1856). During the nineteenth century, the two most prominent European explorer-travelers of the century, John Lewis Burckhardt and Sir Richard Burton, also managed to visit Islam's Holy Cities in disguise and wrote detailed accounts of the pilgrimage.

Upon arriving in Mecca, the pilgrims first go directly to the Sacred Mosque, approaching it while making the following declaration:

> O my Lord, here I am at Your service, here I am. There is no partner with You, here I am. Truly, the praise and the provisions are Yours, and so is the dominion and sovereignty. There is no partner with You. (Mohamed, 1996)

Upon arrival at the Sacred Mosque, the pilgrims perform the circumambulation of the Kaaba seven times in a counter-clockwise direction. The Kaaba, located in the center of the vast open courtyard of the Mosque, is the cube-shaped shrine draped in black cloth. The Kaaba is the most important sanctuary of Islam. It is to Kaaba that the Muslims throughout the world face five times each day when they recite their prayers. The site where the Kaaba is located is, according to the Muslim beliefs, the exact same site where Abraham and Ishmael built and dedicated the first House of the Lord. Within one wall of the Kaaba is embedded the Black Stone, which is believed to be the only extant part of the original House of the Lord. The pilgrims, as they go around the Kaaba seven times, attempt to get a glimpse or get close enough to the shrine so as to touch the silver casing which protects this highly venerated relic.

Following the circumambulation of the Kaaba, the pilgrims proceed to the "hills" of Safa and Marwa where they make seven trips on foot between these "hills." It was here that Hagar and her son Ishmael suffered from extreme thirst. Safa and Marwa are now enclosed and connected by a covered passageway which is next to the Great Mosque. This ritual symbolizes Hagar's desperate search for water in the dry land. The pilgrims then seek to drink the water from the sacred well, which has come to be known by the name of Zamzam, that was revealed to Hagar by Allah. The water from the well of Zamzam is regarded by Muslims as the holiest water. The completion of rites described up to this point would constitute the *umra* or the Little Pilgrimage. The following additional rites would be performed only in conjunction with the Great Pilgrimage.

On the eighth day of the pilgrimage, the entire congregation of the pilgrims proceeds to the valley of Mina, located about six miles outside Mecca. The pilgrims spend the night in the valley in preparation for the next day's ritual at the plain of Arafat, located at a distance of an additional eight miles from Mina. The pilgrims arrive at Arafat around noon and stand in prayer until sundown. It was here that the Prophet Muhammad had delivered his farewell sermon. This phase of the pilgrimage is regarded as the principal event of the *hajj* and has been described as "without doubt the most impressive moment of the pilgrimage" (*The Encyclopedia of Islam*, vol. III, 1979). At sundown, the pilgrims proceed for the return journey to Mecca.

On the way back to Mecca, the pilgrims rest for the night at the town of Muzdalifah, where they also collect small stones for the ceremony of casting seven stones at the devil. This ceremony occurs at the next stop in Mina where the pilgrims cast their stones at three pillars that symbolize the Satan. This ritual recalls the Satan's attempts to dissuade Abraham from obeying God's command to sacrifice Ishmael. Thus the ritual reminds the pilgrims of the struggle against the devil and evil forces, and reinforces their commitment and determination to reject evil thoughts and deeds. The pilgrims then complete the *hajj* by circumambulating the Kaaba seven more times. The final act of the pilgrimage is for the pilgrim to shave the head or cut a lock of hair symbolizing the end of the state of *ihram* or prohibition. Upon the completion of the pilgrimage on the tenth day, the pilgrims, as well as the rest of the Islamic world, celebrate the festival of *Eid al-Adha* (Festival of Sacrifice) which not only concludes the season of the pilgrimage but also celebrates the story of Abraham's willingness to sacrifice his son. Sheep, goats and camels are sacrificed in commemoration, and the meat is shared with the poor. After the completion of rites in and near Mecca, many pilgrims also travel to Medina, two hundred miles to the north and the second holiest town of Islam, to visit the tomb of the Prophet Muhammad.

For devout Muslims, going on the *hajj* represents the journey of a lifetime. The pilgrimage brings a Muslim closest to Allah in this physical world. For those who make the pilgrimage it is a fulfillment of a life-long dream. A vast number of Muslims, however, are not able to fulfill this requirement of their faith because of lack of means. During the nineteenth century it is estimated that from 50,000 to about 200,000 pilgrims performed the *hajj* annually (*The Encyclopedia of Islam*, vol. III, 1979; also see Long, 1979). During the first decade of the twentieth century, the number reached as high as three hundred thousand, but declined considerably during the period between the two World Wars. The decades of the 1940s and the 1950s witnessed growth in the number of pilgrims and by the latter part of this century, the numbers are estimated to have climbed to between one and two million pilgrims. Nigeria has become a leading country of origin for pilgrims. In 1977, over one hundred thousand pilgrims originated in Nigeria, constituting the largest number of pilgrims from a single country (Guellouz, 1979). A leading modern scholar of Islamic civilization has characterized the Islamic pilgrimage as "the most important agency of voluntary, personal mobility before the age of the great European discoveries" (*The Encyclopedia of Islam*, vol. III, 1979). Overall, however, less than one-tenth of one percent of the Muslims worldwide are able to perform the pilgrimage in a given year.

The performance of the pilgrimage is obligatory only if one has the resources to do so. Before embarking on the pilgrimage, the pilgrim must have sufficient resources to pay off his or her debts, provide for himself during the journey, and provide for his family during his absence. Many of the believers who do perform it are fairly old, for it has taken them a lifetime of labor to sacrifice and save enough in order to fulfill this obligation. On the other hand, in the modern world, in many countries, not all the Muslims who are able to afford to go on the pilgrimage are able to travel because of foreign exchange and currency regulations. In these countries lottery drawings are held to select those who could travel to perform these sacred rites. Certain categories of people are exempted from the requirement to perform the pilgrimage. These include the insane, slaves, children and the sick. In the case of the sick and the elderly, the use of a substitute is permissible (*The Encyclopedia of Islam*, vol. III, 1979).

Mansa Musa on Pilgrimage

It is not known exactly when or which peoples of the Western Sudan first went on the pilgrimage to Mecca. The earliest Arabic sources mention the people of ancient Ghana as journeying to perform the pilgrimage sometime in the twelfth century. Abu Hamid al-Gharnati (A.D. 1080-1170), a native of Granada, Spain, provides the earliest reference to the effect that the people of Ghana traveled to Mecca to perform the pilgrimage. Ghana, it will be recalled, had preceded the empire of Mali. In fact, as Mali expanded in size and power, it assimilated the old state of Ghana within its imperial system. Thus, by the time ancient Mali emerged on the scene, the tradition of Western Sudanese Muslims going on the pilgrimage to Mecca was well rooted.

Malian oral traditions and early Arabic written accounts both record the participation in the pilgrimage rituals by several Mansas of Mali before Mansa Musa. However, not many details about the journeys and the experiences of these early Malian rulers are available except for their names and, in some cases, the years when the pilgrimages were undertaken. According to some oral traditions, one Malian ruler, Allakoi Musa, is believed to have performed four pilgrimages to Mecca during the period before the emergence of ancient Mali as an empire under Sundiata in the 1230s (Levtzion, 1979). However, serious doubts have been raised regarding this story. Tall (1977) strongly asserts that Allakoi Musa was not even a ruler of Mali; and, he is not mentioned in any of the Arabic sources.

Three Malian rulers are mentioned in Ibn Khaldun's account as having journeyed to Mecca to perform the pilgrimage. The first of these was Baramandana. No additional information about him is known. Trimingham suggests that Baramandana might not be the name of a ruler, but a title (Trimingham, 1962). The other two pilgrim kings of ancient Mali mentioned by Ibn Khaldun are Mansa Uli, who is said to have ruled between 1255 and 1270, and Mansa Sakura, who ruled between 1285 and 1300.

Mansa Musa's celebrated journey took place in 1324 and must have continued into the following year. Mansa Musa's pilgrimage has been characterized variously by modern scholars as bizarre, fantastic and extraordinary. It was lavish and extravagant. It was the latter qualities that impressed the medieval Arab authors to such an extent that they recorded more details about this particular pilgrimage than the previous ones undertaken by other Western Sudanese rulers. Thanks to their accounts about this particular pilgrimage, Mansa Musa's name has been etched brilliantly in the annals of the medieval history of the African continent.

One of the principal Western Sudanese chroniclers, Mahmud Kati, provides us with a possible motive that led Mansa Musa to undertake the *hajj*. In his chronicle, the *Tarikh al-Fattash,* written in the sixteenth century, Kati informs us that another local scholar by the name of Muhammad Quma had related that Mansa Musa had accidentally killed his mother, Nana Kankan, as a result of which Mansa Musa suffered great anguish and became greatly worried about divine punishment. Subsequently, he sought the advice of a learned Muslim theologian as to how he could achieve or obtain repentance for this act. The theologian suggested that the Mansa should submit himself to the protection of the Prophet Muhammad and seek his intervention with Allah for forgiveness (Lewis, 1974). Based upon this advice, according to Kati, the Mansa decided that same day to prepare for the pilgrimage. It must be noted that Kati's account is the only one that mentions this episode. None of the Egyptian officials who had met the Mansa or who wrote about his stay in that country made any reference to the Mansa's grief or being troubled by having caused the death of his mother. Later in his text, Kati stated that there were many stories about Mansa Musa's journey, most of which were untrue. Therefore, it is difficult to determine which, if any, of these stories are an accurate portrayal of events.

Having decided to perform the pilgrimage, the Mansa is said to have sent out a call throughout his empire for supplies that were necessary for the long journey. Another Muslim countryman advised him that the journey should commence, for an unexplained reason, only on a Saturday that also was the twelfth day of the month. The Mansa followed this advice as well and awaited his departure until this condition was met which happened, according to Levtzion (1983), nine months later. Since then, traveling on a Saturday which also happened to be the twelfth day of the month came to be regarded as a lucky omen among the people of Mali according to Kati.

While many details about the journey across the Sahara Desert are not recorded, two aspects of the journey have been underscored in most of the surviving accounts. These relate to the size of the Mansa's party and the amount of gold that was taken along and spent. Regarding the size of Mansa Musa's entourage, there are widely different numbers found in the sources. Mahmud Kati informs us in the *Tarikh al-Fattash* that eight thousand people accompanied the Mansa. As-Sadi, the author of *Tarikh as-Sudan*, another renowned chronicle about and from the Western Sudan, informs us that the entourage of Mansa Musa was made up of sixty thousand people. Ibn Khatir, writing in the 1350s, mentioned that there were twenty thousand people in the entourage. Al-Muammar Al-Kumi, who joined up with Mansa Musa's entourage in the town of Ghadames (about halfway between Egypt and Mali) during the Mansa's return journey reported, according to Al-Umari, that about twelve thousand slave women, dressed in Yemeni silk, were part of the Mansa's party carrying his supplies and furnishings (Levtzion & Hopkins, 1981). All we can say for certain, I suppose, is that there were thousands of people who went along with Mansa Musa on his historic journey. Family members, nobles, soldiers, slaves, merchants, theologians and average fellow countrymen from all corners of the empire must have formed the entourage. His wife, Inari Kunate, was also in the entourage. This is one of the very rare references made in the records about a royal wife.

Leaving the realm behind to the custody of his son, Mansa Musa set out on his pilgrimage from his capital of Niani and traveled northwest toward Walata (As-Sadi, 1964). Walata, it will be recalled, was the first Malian town that Ibn Battuta entered during his travels through the Western Sudan in the early 1350s where he had stayed for about fifty days. He had described it as quite a hot place, mostly inhabited by the Massufa Berbers, and where people wore fine clothes made out of fabrics imported from Egypt. From Walata the Mansa's party traveled northeast to Tuat, another major center in the trans-Saharan trade network. In Tuat, according to As-Sadi, Mansa Musa left behind many members of his party who suffered from some illness that affected their feet—perhaps swollen feet or some similar malady. The journey continued for several weeks across the Algerian and Libyan deserts until the group's arrival in Cairo.

Besides the large size of the party that accompanied him, the Mansa gained fame due to the large quantity of gold that he had brought along. Early records mention eighty to one hundred loads of gold weighing nearly two thousand pounds that was taken along for expenses.

The Mansa Musa entourage entered Cairo near the famed pyramids. What Mansa Musa thought about these ancient African monuments is not known. Upon arrival in the Egyptian capital, according to Ibn Khaldun, he extended his courtesy to the Mamluk Sultan, Al-Malik Al-Nasir, by sending rich presents to him including fifty thousand dinars (gold coins). Ibn Khatir recorded that the Malian delegation carried so much gold with it that the value of gold dropped in the Egyptian market and, as Al-Umari also recorded later, it remained low for several years. Ibn Khatir also informs us that when Mansa Musa came to Egypt, he was a "young, handsome man" (Levtzion & Hopkins, 1981). The Malians were accommodated in encampments in the Qarafa section of Old Cairo where the Sultan of Egypt owned a residence which he gave as a gift to Mansa Musa. We have a brief description of this neighborhood of Cairo as it appeared in the 1320s in the accounts of Ibn Battuta. He stated, "At Cairo too is the great cemetery of al-Qarafa, which is place of peculiar sanctity, and contains the graves of innumerable scholars and pious believers. In the Qarafa the people build beautiful pavilions surrounded by walls, so that they look like houses" (Ibn Battuta, 1969).

Shortly after his arrival in Cairo, Mansa Musa reluctantly met with the ruler of Egypt who at the time was Sultan Al-Malik Al-Nasir. This famous meeting between Mansa Musa and the Sultan of Egypt has been described earlier. It will be recalled that at this meeting between the two powerful Muslim sovereigns, Mansa Musa refused to kiss the ground and bow down to the Egyptian ruler. In any event, the two rulers are said to have gotten along well. They exchanged many gifts. Egypt at the time was dominated by the Mamluk dynasty which had overthrown the previous dynasty, known as the Ayyubid, in A.D.1250. Mansa Musa's two predecessors, Mansa Uli and Mansa Sakura, who are known to have made the pilgrimages, also most likely passed through Cairo and performed their pilgrimages during the reigns of the Mamluk sultans. The Mamluk dynasty was the most powerful dynasty in North Africa and the Middle East. In the middle of the 1200s, the Muslim world had suffered major defeats at the hands of the Mongols. The Mamluk rulers of Egypt had successfully halted the Mongol expansion in the region and, by the end of the 1200s, had emerged as a powerful force in the region. The Mamluk rulers were also engaged in wars involving the European crusaders and they were successful in forcing the crusaders out of several parts of the region. The Mamluks were also notable because they had risen up from the ranks of the slave soldiers. Thus Egypt under the Mamluks was a powerful state whose control extended as far as Syria and the Levant. The Holy Cities of Mecca and Medina were under the patronage and guardianship of the Mamluk rulers although they faced some challenges from the sultans of Yemen. Mansa Uli undertook his pilgrimage during the reign of Mamluk Sultan Baybars I, and Mansa Sakura and Mansa Musa journeyed during the reign of Sultan Al-Malik Al-Nasir. It is reasonable to speculate that during Mansa Musa's meeting with the Egyptian sultan, conversation must have included the topics of the wars with the Mongols and the crusaders.

It is not known what Mansa Musa's impressions were about Cairo or Egypt. Ibn Battuta, who first arrived in Cairo just a couple of years after Mansa Musa's pilgrimage, has left a very flowery description of Cairo in the 1320s. He stated that Cairo was the "mother of cities and seat of Pharaoh the tyrant, mistress of broad regions and fruitful lands, boundless in multitude of buildings, peerless in beauty and splendor, the meeting-place of feeble and mighty, whose throngs surge as the waves of the sea, and can scarce be contained in her for all her size and capacity" (Ibn Battuta, 1969).

Mansa Musa in one account is said to have stayed in Egypt for one year before continuing the journey to the Holy Cities (see Al-Dawadari in Levtzion & Hopkins, 1981). While in Cairo Mansa Musa consistently maintained a spiritual demeanor and performed many acts of charity and displayed much generosity and kindness. His entourage was described as well mannered, well dressed and dignified. When the time for the departure to the Holy Cities came, the Sultan of Egypt is said to have sent additional gifts to Mansa Musa and supplied his entourage with camels, equipment and adequate supplies for the journey. The sultan is also said to have arranged for the deposits of supplies along the route for the large caravan. In addition, the sultan instructed the caravan commander to treat the Malian ruler with honor and dignity.

While we do not have many specific details about Mansa Musa's particular journey from Cairo to Mecca, there are accounts from earlier and later travelers, including Ibn Battuta, who provide us some insights to the logistics and arrangements involved in the journey between Cairo and Mecca. F. E. Peters, in his book, *The Hajj: The Muslim Pilgrimage to Mecca and the Holy Places* (1994), has gathered a great many of these accounts. Based upon these accounts, the following general description about Mansa Musa's journey to Mecca has been compiled.

The caravans that set out from Mecca were under the command of an *amir al-hajj* (commander of the pilgrims' caravan). We know from the early accounts that as Mansa Musa's entourage prepared to set out from Cairo, the Egyptian sultan Al-Malik al-Nasir instructed the commander of the caravan to honor and treat Mansa Musa with dignity. It was the commander's task to organize the details of the caravan which surely must have been a very challenging task, especially considering that Mansa Musa's entourage may have included close to sixty thousand pilgrims. The commander of the caravan was expected to arrange for the collection and distribution of the necessary supplies for the journey; try to assure the safety of the pilgrims during the journey; and assure the safe delivery of donations contributed for the Holy Cities (Peters, 1994a). The Mamluk rulers also sent with the caravan commander the *kiswa* (the black embroidered cloth that was draped over the Kaaba). The pilgrims were organized in certain order and were expected to remain within their assigned or designated sections and not break the rank.

Upon leaving Cairo, the caravan traveled eastward across the Sinai Peninsula passing through Suez. Then it turned southwards and followed the western coastline of Arabia along the Red Sea. The journey between Cairo and Mecca lasted about forty days each way. The distance of about one thousand miles was covered in thirty-four segments, each one covering a distance of about thirty miles. A good portion of the travel was done during the night hours. The journey would be somewhat more difficult and fatiguing in the intense heat of the daytime. The caravan passed through several important towns and villages such as Madyan, al-Wadjh, Yanbu and Rabigh (Peters, 1994a). Rabigh was a short distance to the north from Mecca. There the caravan from Egypt sometimes linked up with caravans coming from Syria, Iraq and Iran. Ibn Battuta, who journeyed to Mecca from Syria in 1326, informs us that it was in Rabigh that the pilgrims coming from Egypt would put on their pilgrims' garments and enter into the state of *Ihram*. According to Ibn Battuta, Rabigh was located in a valley that was wellwatered from the rains which left behind pools for long periods of time. From Rabigh to Mecca was a short distance that was covered in just a few days. During this last segment, the pilgrims passed through a fertile area which supplied lots of fruits and vegetables to Mecca (Ibn Battuta, 1969).

While in Mecca, Mansa Musa performed all the rites and rituals associated with the Great Pilgrimage. Muhanna al-Urjumi was the guide who attended to Mansa Musa. Al-Umari informs us that he learned from the guide not only the fact that Mansa Musa completed the pilgrimage but also that the Malian ruler was very generous towards the pilgrims and the residents of the Holy City. He distributed much wealth in the city. The guide reported that he was given about two hundred mithqals (about twenty-five ounces) of gold by the Malian ruler. The guide further stated that during the journey Mansa Musa and his companions dressed up in magnificent clothes.

As in the case of Mansa Musa's stay in Cairo, we do not have much information about the Malian ruler's thoughts or impressions about his stay in the Holy City of Mecca. It must have been one of his most emotional and exhilarating experiences. He and the members of his entourage must have felt a great sense of accomplishment, especially bearing in mind the hardships of the journey. Even some of the European Christian travelers who managed to visit Mecca in disguise expressed experiencing a variety of peak emotional experiences. As to the condition of Islam's most sacred city and its inhabitants around the time of Mansa Musa's sojourn there, we get some glimpses from the account of Ibn Battuta, who arrived in Mecca a little under two years after Mansa Musa's visit. We can safely assume that not a great deal changed in Mecca between the visits of Mansa Musa and Ibn Battuta. Ibn Battuta described the residents of Mecca as kind to strangers and generous towards the poor and the less fortunate. Apparently there were many poor people in the city who depended for their survival on generous handouts from the well-to-do members of the community. He described the presence of many orphan children who performed menial tasks to earn their living. The prosperous Meccans were described as elegantly dressed in white clothes and well perfumed. The use of perfume which is prohibited during the *hajj* was widely used otherwise. Ibn Battuta observed that people might even go hungry for a night in order to be able to afford some perfume.

Besides its principal religious purpose, the pilgrimage in Mecca has also served other functions. It has always had a great commercial impact. The convergence of thousands and thousands of people during the pilgrimage gave rise to many opportunities to enterprising individuals to profit by providing services and by engaging in trade. Combining legitimate commerce with the pilgrimage was and is quite permissible. As pronounced in the Quran (Sura 2:198):

> It is no crime in you if ye seek of the bounty of your
> Lord (during pilgrimage)...

Thus, trade and commerce flourished as a consequence of the pilgrimage. Peters (1994a) has described the commercial aspect of the pilgrimage in the following terms: "It was from the earliest times an annual fair, a merchandising opportunity of the first magnitude, and not only at Jidda (the major Arabian port city) and Mecca but even upon the road." In fact, engaging in commerce was one way to earn the necessary means to pay for the expenses of the *hajj*. Petty traders as well as those involved in large-scale business enterprises found ample opportunities. Several extant accounts shed light on the merchandise that many of the pilgrims brought along with them. A sixteenth century account lists silk, a variety of grains, precious stones and metal products among items carried by traders. John Lewis Burckhardt, one of the Europeans who managed to travel to Mecca in the nineteenth century, observed a much wider range of commodities. These included bonnets and cloaks from Northwest Africa; footwear, pastries, purses, embroidered cloth, shawls, silk, and carpets from Turkey; toothbrushes and stone beads from Afghanistan; silks and cashmere shawls from Persia; and other items from Yemen and India. The only type of commodity that Burckhardt noted that the Africans brought were articles used in the slave trade (Peters, 1994a).

The *hajj* experience has also served and continues to serve to increase the zeal and commitment of the pilgrims to the faith. This in turn has led many individuals to change the course of their lives, and sometimes the course of history of their community following the pilgrimage. In the 1960s we saw how the life of Malcolm X and the history of the Nation of Islam took a different turn following his journey to Mecca. In the eleventh century, Abdullah Ibn Yassin experienced a major transformation in his religious attitude that ultimately led him to found the Almoravid movement, which in turn greatly impacted the history of Northwest Africa and parts of the Western Sudan as discussed in earlier chapters of this work. With respect to Mansa Musa, one account informs us that Mansa Musa experienced such a powerful religious awakening during the *hajj* that he is said to have decided to abdicate the throne of Mali upon his return to his homeland and then to go back to live in Mecca.

Another important function that is served by the pilgrimage is that it affords a unique opportunity to the pilgrims to meet and get acquainted with their co-religionists from many different parts of the world. It is the occasion when the *ummah* (the global Islamic community) comes together. For most of the pilgrims during most of the pilgrimages, this gathering of the *ummah* has to be largely symbolic in nature. The short duration of stay in the Holy Cities and a fast-paced schedule of rites and rituals to be accomplished would not allow much free time to build too many lasting relationships with co-religionists from diverse parts of the Islamic world. Also, the differences in languages would pose insurmountable obstacles to building long-lasting friendships and relationships among co-religionists from different parts of the world.

However, in the case of Mansa Musa, the accounts inform us that during his stay in Mecca he did establish friendships with several other Muslims from different parts of the Islamic world. It is also indicated in the Egyptian accounts that Mansa Musa was fluent in the Arabic language which must have greatly facilitated his interactions with pilgrims from the Arabic-speaking realms. Mansa Musa invited some of the people he met in Mecca to travel to Mali with him. The most notable of these pilgrims with whom Mansa Musa became acquainted during his sojourn in Mecca was As-Saheli, the renowned poet and architect from Spain. As-Saheli came from a well-to-do family of Granada. He accompanied Mansa Musa to Mali and is credited with having built the Great Mosque in Timbuktu, a mosque in Gao, and a palace for the Mansa. As-Saheli later died in Timbuktu where Ibn Battuta visited his tomb in the 1350s. Several scholars belonging to the Maliki school of jurisprudence are also reported to have accompanied Mansa Musa to Mali. Mansa Musa also enticed four descendants of the Prophet Muhammad's Quraysh tribe to settle in Mali (Levtzion, 1980).

Disagreement among various sources exists as to the length of time that Mansa Musa remained in Mecca. Some say he remained for days; others say he stayed as long as three months. On the return journey, his entourage passed through the city of Medina where they visited the Prophet's tomb. For part of the return journey back to Cairo, according to Ibn Khaldun, Mansa Musa and his group became separated from the main caravan but eventually managed to rejoin the caravan and reached Cairo safely. However, according to other sources, many members of the entourage and camels succumbed to the cold and died.

Upon Mansa Musa's return to Cairo from Arabia, the Malian ruler was again well received by the Egyptian Sultan. The Egyptian official who welcomed the Mansa back from Mecca reported that the Sultan conferred honors upon him, provided accommodations and presented him with many gifts consisting of Alexandrian cloth and other precious items (Levtzion & Hopkins, 1981). It was apparently during this second stay in Cairo that the Mansa's financial situation took a bizarre turn. As pointed out in an earlier chapter, the early written accounts inform us that Mansa

Musa had initially set out from Mali with eighty to one hundred loads of gold, approximately two thousand pounds in weight, to pay for the expenses. Most of this wealth was spent by the time the entourage returned to Cairo from Mecca. The sources have indicated that whatever was left was lavishly spent in the bazaars of Cairo. It seems that the Mansa and his entourage bought everything in sight. And, in addition, the sources inform us that the merchants of Cairo charged the Malian shoppers exorbitant prices—charging them as much as five times the normal prices. The merchants are said to have made big profits. The Malians soon ran out of their wealth and Mansa Musa found himself in the position of a borrower. He obtained loans from a number of the leading merchants of Cairo. Ibn Khaldun informs us that the Al-Kuwayk family, a wealthy merchant family, lent him fifty thousand *dinars* (currency in the form of gold coins common in many Muslim countries). Mansa Musa is also said to have sold the palace which was given to him as a gift by the Sultan of Egypt with the Sultan's permission. The Malians also resold some of the goods that they had purchased but at reduced prices. There are conflicting accounts about the repayment of the loans borrowed by the Malians which, according to Al-Umari, had been provided at a very high premium. These dealings are described below.

Mansa Musa and his entourage departed from Cairo sometime in 1325. During the return journey across the Sahara Desert, the entourage passed through what are today the countries of Libya and Niger. Along the way, the Malian emperor was joined at Ghadames (modern Libya), about halfway between Egypt and Mali, by a regional leader named Al-Muammar who wanted Mansa Musa's help in a conflict that he, Al-Muammar, was involved in with another leader. Al-Muammar accompanied Mansa Musa to the latter's capital city and he praised the Mansa for having accorded him extremely friendly treatment. Al-Muammar further reported that Mansa Musa had brought along so much equipment and furnishings that it took twelve thousand women slaves to carry it all (Levtzion & Hopkins, 1981).

Mansa Musa's dire financial situation towards the end of his stay in Cairo apparently did not tarnish his image or reputation. On the contrary, his generosity in giving away a good portion of his wealth and his entourage's extravagant shopping sprees earned him an everlasting recognition in the annals of African history. In the words of one modern author, "It was the pilgrimage that awakened the world to the stupendous wealth of Mali" (*The Encyclopedia of Islam*, vol. VIII, 1995). His fame spread not only across the Islamic world but also to parts of Europe where cartographers and map-makers of the fourteenth century began to include references to Mali and the Mansa of Mali in their maps for the first time. The first reference to Mali in a European map was made in 1339 by the Genoese cartographer Angelino Dulcert. A more renowned reference to Mansa Musa and Mali appeared in the Majorcan Atlas of Abraham Cresques in 1375 (see p.118). Cresque's *Catalan Atlas* is regarded as a masterpiece of the Majorcan school of cartographers and was produced for King Peter III of Aragon who presented it to King Charles V of France (Skelton, 1964). The famous atlas contains a drawing of a Malian king wearing a golden crown and holding up a nugget of gold. An accompanying inscription describes Mansa Musa as the richest and the noblest king in the Western Sudan.

Regarding the repayment of loans borrowed by Mansa Musa from lenders in Cairo, an account written in the 1330s by Al-Dawadari stated that the lenders lost out and did not receive any repayments (Levtzion & Hopkins, 1981). Al-Umari, also writing in the 1330s, informs us that after Mansa Musa had returned to his homeland following the pilgrimage, the Sultan of Egypt received a letter from Mansa Musa conveying greetings to the Sultan of Egypt and about four hundred ounces of gold as a gift. Whether this gold was to repay any of the loans is not stated. Ibn Khaldun, writing in the 1390s, about seventy years after the pilgrimage, informs us that Siraj Al-Din Al-Kuwayk, one of the lenders, had sent one of his agents along with Mansa Musa on his return trip to Mali for the purpose of collecting debt. However, the agent died during the journey. Al-Kuwayk then sent another agent and one of his sons. The second agent also died, but the son did receive a portion of the payment and returned to Cairo. Ibn Battuta, who visited Mali in the early 1350s, confirmed in his account that the son received the repayment, apparently the full amount, and returned to Egypt. But, according to Ibn Khaldun, Mansa Musa still owed debt to some of the lenders and this remained unpaid due to Mansa Musa's death. Finally, an account written by Ibn Hajar in the 1390s stated that upon his return to Mali, Mansa Musa repaid all his debts.

In any case, Mansa Musa's pilgrimage made a great impression in Egypt and beyond. It came to be regarded in Egypt as one of the major events of the year. Mansa Musa elevated the reputation of ancient Mali as not only a major Western Sudanese kingdom but also as one of the largest kingdoms in the world. Modern day historians and writers also acknowledge him as a most important personality of African history. Davidson (1965) characterizes Mansa Musa as "one of the greatest statesman in the history of Africa." A recent special issue of the *Life* magazine (Fall 1997) entitled "The Millennium" and featuring one hundred events and one hundred personalities that changed the world between A.D. 1001 and 1999 recognized Mansa Musa's pilgrimage among the most important events of the millennium. A few authors, however, suggest that his actual contribution is probably exaggerated. However, the pilgrimage contributed much to the Islamization of Mali's ruling elite and the spread of Islamic learning and scholarship within Mali. This scholarly tradition was carried to even greater heights in the empire of Songhay that succeeded ancient Mali.

Although Mansa Musa ruled ancient Mali when the empire was at its political and economic peak, and although he gained such widespread fame in the outside world, his position and status in the local traditions is lower than that of Sundiata, the founder of the empire of ancient Mali. While Sundiata is celebrated through a number of versions of the "Sundiata epic," no epics have developed among the Malinke people to celebrate the accomplishments of Mansa Musa (Johnson, 1992). The pilgrimage itself, however, inspired the development of the Fajigi legend in the Malian oral tradition which indicates that the legendary Fajigi (described in the tradition as the father of hope) traveled to Mecca and upon his return introduced certain symbols that became part of the traditional religion of the people (*The Encyclopedia of Islam*, vol. VI, 1991). Mansa Musa, it appears, became more a beloved figure in the Arab and Islamic world than in his homeland. His twenty-five year reign came to an end with his death in 1337. Within a few years afterward, Mali entered a period of decline and was eventually, at least partially, taken over by the empire of Songhay, the third most renowned medieval empire of Western Sudan. The decline of ancient Mali is discussed in some detail in the final chapter of this work.

Mansa Musa as portrayed in the Catalan Atlas of 1375

CHAPTER VI

THE SLAVE TRADE

Introduction

As discussed in the earlier chapters, ancient Mali, from the late thirteenth century, had established close trade links with the Islamic world, especially with North Africa. The slave trade became an important aspect of the larger trade relationship between the Western Sudan and the Islamic regions of North Africa and the Middle East. Thus, any substantial discussion of the history of the relationship between Islam and Africa or Africans would be incomplete without including the topic of slavery and slave trade because the institution of slavery eventually constituted a major strand in that relationship. While integrating the small amount of information available in the early records concerning the institution of slavery as it existed in ancient Mali, particularly during the reign of Mansa Musa, this chapter will explore the larger topic of Islam, Muslims and the African slave trade.

In exploring the relationship between Islam and the African slave trade, this chapter will focus, in particular, upon the following themes in general—(i) Islam's theological teachings regarding the institution of slavery: that is to say, how the Quran, the *hadith* and the *shariah* deal with the subject of slavery; (ii) the role played by the Muslims in the conduct of the slave trade with West Africa; (iii) the conditions and treatment of slaves in the Islamic environment; (iv) the size and magnitude of the trade; (v) the emancipation and the abolition of slavery and the slave trade in the Islamic regions; and finally, (vi) how the slave trade and slavery impacted Africa and Africans.

The primary focus of this chapter is slave trade as it occurred across the Sahara Desert and as it involved and impacted the peoples and states of the Western Sudan. Nubia (southern Egypt and northern Sudan), Ethiopia, Somalia and East Africa were other regions of the continent that were intimately linked in the Islamic world's trade in human beings, but these are given only passing references in the present study. Since only meager details are contained in the fourteenth century sources and other earlier sources regarding slave trade with the Western Sudan, the author will also synthesize wherever appropriate details about the trans-

Saharan slave trade contained in the accounts of later writers, especially several nineteenth century explorers. This chapter is designed to serve only as an introduction to the topic of Islam and slavery. Readers seeking more detailed analyses of the subject are referred to the excellent contributions of Bernard Lewis, John R. Wills, Humphrey J. Fisher, and others. These authors, through their translations of the Arabic texts and diligent research in the archives of the medieval Islamic world, have vastly increased our understanding of the practice of this most oppressive of human institutions as it occurred in the Islamic civilization. Still, literature dealing with Islam and the African slave trade represents only a fraction of that dealing with the Atlantic slave trade.

Islam on Slavery

The institution of slavery is as old as recorded history. Its existence is recorded in many of the renowned civilizations of antiquity. The civilizations of ancient Mesopotamia, Egypt, Greece and Rome are some of the major examples of civilizations in which slavery was an important cultural component. Slavery has been almost a permanent part of the human society. Milton Meltzer in his book *Slavery: A World History* (1993) provides an excellent introduction to and survey of the practice of slavery from antiquity to modern times. While its practice has differed from one civilization to another, its underlying assumptions have remained constant—the ownership of one human being by another human being and the associated practice of buying and selling human beings. And, even though most assume that slavery is an institution of the past, slavery is not a totally eradicated institution from the present day world. Numerous human rights watch groups annually issue reports that describe its continued existence in several regions of the world. Although slavery was practiced in many civilizations throughout the course of human history, it is said to have been of particular significance in the advancement of two of the most important civilizations of the world—the Western Civilization of which we in the United States are a part and the Islamic Civilization (*New Encyclopedia Britannica*, vol. 27, 1992).

Slavery was also an integral part of the Arabian landscape prior to the advent of Islam. The pre-Islamic slavery in Arabia was not confined to Africans. Various non-African groups of people were also obtained as slaves. A vast majority of the African slaves in pre-Islamic Arabia, however, most likely originated from the nearby lands of Ethiopia, the Horn of Africa and East Africa. Thus, slavery was a major feature of the Arabian culture during the time of the Prophet Muhammad and the Prophet himself is said to have owned slaves. In his early efforts to attract adherents, the Prophet Muhammad offered freedom to the slaves who embraced the new religion. As a result, many slaves are said to have converted to Islam. A number of these former slaves played an important part in the growth and expansion of the Islamic faith during and after the time of the Prophet Muhammad. The most famous such slave who converted was Bilal, who was a son of an Ethiopian slave woman. Bilal eventually became a close companion of the Prophet and became the first *muezzin* (prayer caller) of Islam.

Although the institution of slavery not only continued to exist but expanded phenomenally under Islam, the advent of Islam interjected many new rules and injunctions regarding the practice of slavery. Soon after its establishment Islam became one of the largest imperial cultures the world had ever known. Its power and institutions impacted a diverse array of peoples who fell within its domination.

With the successful establishment of Islam in Arabia, the culture of the land underwent important changes. From this point onward, Muslims had to be in accordance with the Quran for any activity in which they engaged. The Quran served as the primary source for determining rightful and sinful acts. The *hadith* of the Prophet provided additional guidance with regard to what is right and wrong. With regard to the institution of slavery, neither the Quran nor the *hadith* explicitly prohibit its practice. On the other hand, neither do they encourage its practice. Basically, the Quran and the *hadith* state that slavery is an allowable practice and provide some mandates and guidance on how it should be practiced. In Islam the practice of slavery is not considered a sinful activity.

The acceptance and tolerance of the institution of slavery in the Quran is indicated by the presence of several verses which assume the existence of slavery and regulate its practice. The most important of these verses which are regarded as permitting slavery include the following:

> Alms are for the poor and the needy and those employed to administer the (funds); for those whose hearts have been (recently) reconciled (to truth); for those *in bondage* and in debt; in the cause of Allah; and for the way-farer; (thus is it) ordained by Allah

and Allah is full of knowledge and wisdom. (Sura 9:60)

The above verse has been interpreted to mean that Islam is not against the condition of bondage. However, it places an obligation on the community to help take care of those in bondage. The following verse has been interpreted to not only allow for Muslims to possess or own other human beings but also confirms the inequality between master and the slave.

> Allah has bestowed His gifts of sustenance more freely on some of you than others; those more favored are not going to throw back their gifts to those whom their right hands possess so as to be equal in that respect. Will they then deny the favors of Allah? (Sura 16:71)

Another verse, Sura 24:58, prescribes how slaves should approach their masters when the latter are praying or dressing and undressing. Another important verse that acknowledges the existence of the status of slavery is a verse about marriage. This is an interesting verse because it gives the slave a higher status than a free person if the slave is a believer and the free person is a non-believer. The verse states:

> Do not marry unbelieving women until they believe; a slavewoman who believes is better than an unbelieving woman even though she allure you. Nor marry (your girls) to unbelievers until they believe; a man slave who believes is better than an unbeliever even though he allure you... (Sura 2:221)

Thus, it is through references to slaves such as indicated in the above verses that it is recognized that Islam does not prohibit the practice of slavery. The Islamic view has been that whatever is permitted by Allah and His Prophet is right and decent. While legitimizing the institution of slavery, the Quran and the *hadith* also provided advisories and guidance related to the rights, treatment and the emancipation of slaves. And as the Islamic civilization, particularly its jurisprudence, evolved over the centuries, the various schools of law also further refined the rules and regulations governing slavery and the slave trade. These laws, affecting both the slaves and the masters, are explained in detail below in the appropriate sections. At this point, it is useful to describe some of the important general characteristics of Islamic slavery and slave trade.

The principal cause or justification in Islam for enslavement was non-belief in the Islamic religion or paganism. The Islamic world view, like the worldviews of numerous other major civilizations and religions, was and is based on the belief that the world is divided into two groups—Muslims and non-Muslims. Therefore, ideally, the only people who could be rightfully enslaved in Islam had to be non-believers. Christians and Jews were regarded, like Muslims, as the "peoples of the book" and, consequently, were not to be enslaved. A special tax, known as *jizya*, was levied against them. However, the reality was often quite different. Numerous examples of Muslims enslaving the exempted groups are to be found in the historical literature. Also, numerous examples of Muslims enslaving other Muslims, a prohibited activity, can be found in the historical literature.

Another important characteristic of Islamic slavery was that slavery in Islam was not linked to any particular racial group. Slaves in the Muslim world came from diverse racial and ethnic backgrounds. The Quran contains no endorsement in any way to the idea of the existence of any superior or inferior race or races, nor does it pre-ordain any particular race to the condition of slavery. According to Lewis (1990), "At no time did Muslim theologians or jurists accept the idea that there may be races of mankind predisposed by nature or foredoomed by providence to the condition of slavery." However, as Lewis and other authors have pointed out, ideas reflecting racist views did find expression in the writings of several prominent Muslim philosophers and thinkers. Negative stereotypes about the black African people can be found in the Arabic literature.

Finally, just as the slaves in the Islamic world came from diverse racial and ethnic backgrounds, so did the Muslim slave traders and slave owners. There exists a common perception when discussing the subject of Islam and slavery that slavery primarily involved the Arabs as slavers and the Africans as slaves. The truth of the matter is that there were Muslims other than the Arabs who were also quite active as slavers. These included the Berbers, Africans, Turks, Persians and Indians. In the West African slave trade, along with the Arabs, the Muslim Berbers and Muslim Africans played a crucial part in all aspects of the institution of slavery—gathering, selling, buying, transporting and owning slaves. During the Ottoman domination of Egypt and the Nile Valley from the mid-1500s, the Turks also played a key part as slavers, particularly along the Nile.

Conquests and enslavement went hand in hand during the early centuries of Islamic expansion. Slavery was already a common institution in many of the conquered territories, and many of the conquered peoples were considered to be pagans by the Arabs and therefore could legitimately be enslaved. Contrary to popular view, many of the early Islamic conquests were undertaken not for the purpose of spreading Islam but were more motivated by the promise of economic gain and booty, both material and human. Uqba b. Nafi, a major Arab conqueror of North Africa during the seventh century, repeatedly imposed a levy of hundreds of slaves upon the various defeated peoples of North Africa.

Trans-Saharan Slave Trade

In this section we shall explore the development of the slave trade between the peoples and states of the Western Sudan and the wider Islamic world, particularly North Africa and the Middle East. Slave trade across the Sahara Desert is said to have existed for centuries prior to the emergence and expansion of Islam. However, the volume of this traffic is believed to have been fairly small. Black African prisoners of wars and slaves are known to have been present in ancient Greece (Snowden, 1970). Romans may have even waged military campaigns as far south in the Sahara as the Lake Chad region.

The Islamic conquest of North Africa significantly transformed the political, economic and cultural landscapes of the region. Initially, a large number of Berbers who were defeated by the Arab armies satisfied the Arab demand for slaves. However, with the completion of the conquest of North Africa and with the increased conversions of Berbers to Islam, this source of supply of slaves gradually diminished. Increasingly the focus shifted to the lands and peoples across the Sahara to the south as new sources for slaves.

The Islamic expansion in North Africa greatly impacted the nature of economic relations between North Africa and the Western Sudan. The magnitude of trade across the Sahara experienced a vast expansion. The slave trade soon became a major feature of this relationship. Trade soon surpassed the other principal ways—conquest, tribute, and birth to slave parents—in which slaves were obtained in the Islamic world. Many authors suggest that the slave trade, along with trade in gold, became the defining characteristic of the trans-Saharan commerce.

In the earlier centuries after the Arab conquests of North Africa (seventh to eleventh centuries), the Arab settlers and traders constituted a minority. Therefore, the Berbers became the most important link in the expansion of trade across the Sahara. Their familiarity with and the mastery of the Sahara Desert gave them a commanding position in the control of the trans-Saharan trade, including the slave trade. Savage (1992) suggests that by about the middle of the eighth century, the Berbers of the Ibadi sect (a Muslim sect that was in opposition to the mainstream Sunni authority) developed a monopoly in slave trade between parts of the Western Sudan and North Africa.

One of the questions regarding slavery and slave trade in Western Africa that is of academic interest is related to whether external intervention gave rise to these institutions in West Africa or whether these institutions existed indigenously and the native populations merely connected with high external demands for their own greater profits (Fage, 1969). While this question may not be answerable, the early records inform us about the existence of slavery and the slave trade in the Western Sudan both prior to and since the advance of Islamic influence across the Sahara.

One of the earliest references in the post-Islamic era that links slave trade and West Africa is from the account of Al-Yaqubi (late ninth century), who wrote that the kings of the Sudan sold their own people into slavery (Levtzion & Hopkins, 1981). He further states that these kings sold the slaves to the Ibadi Berbers, who then fed them into the markets of Islamic North Africa and further east. Al-Bakri, writing in the 1060s, informs us of the presence of Western Sudanese slaves, particularly women cooks, in the town of Awdaghust in ancient Ghana. Al-Bakri also informs us that slavery was not limited to black Africans. Beautiful, white-complexioned women were also among the slaves in Awdaghust. He describes in quite graphic terms the sexuality of these women slaves. In the 1100s, Al-Zuhuri provided some details about the slave trade from the ancient empire of Ghana. Ralph Austen has estimated that between the mid-600s and 1100 a little over two million slaves were traded across the Sahara (quoted in Phillips, 1985). By the time of the emergence of ancient Mali in the 1200s, the slave trade can be said to have become a tradition. Moreover, as explained in an earlier chapter, Mali's major international linkages were with the Islamic north. Therefore, these factors further served to facilitate the slave trade between the Western Sudan and North Africa and beyond. The next section summarizes the details about the existence of slavery and slave trade in ancient Mali contained in the early Arabic sources.

Ancient Mali and the Slave Trade

In ancient Mali slavery and the slave trade were important elements in both the domestic culture as well as in external trade. Slaves were obtained for a variety of reasons for the domestic use —the most important being for agricultural purposes, mining needs, household and sexual purposes. Some of these reasons were also important in the external demand (discussed in more detail later). Ibn Battuta, who visited Mali in the 1350s, is our most important source regarding the existence and practice of slavery in ancient Mali. He encountered slaves soon after crossing the Sahara Desert in the area of Taghaza. Taghaza was a major salt mining region, and Ibn Battuta informs us that all the workers there were slaves belonging to the Massufa tribe. It must be noted that Taghaza was not a part of Mali but was located at a distance of ten days' journey from its border.

As Ibn Battuta traveled to the capital of Mali and other parts of the kingdom, he made more references to slavery. In describing the scene of a royal assembly in Niani, he mentions the presence of about three hundred slaves in the royal procession of Mansa Sulayman. He also mentions that the principal royal interpreter, the *Dugha*, was accompanied at the assembly by his four wives and about one hundred slave-girls.

In one of the towns of Mali whose name he could not recall, he informs us that during a visit to the local governor's residence, the governor presented him a young boy to keep as a slave to serve him. During the same visit, Ibn Battuta informs us that he met one of the slave-girls of the governor who was an Arab girl from Damascus who conversed with him in Arabic. This is one of the rare references about the presence of non-African slaves in the retinues of Africans. Mansa Musa is said to have purchased and brought back to Mali a certain number of Turkish slaves from Egypt. The number of such foreign slaves that were owned by the Western Sudanese are not cited in any of the sources. Finally, Ibn Battuta informs us that the people of Mali sometimes rivaled with one another regarding the number of slaves they owned and that they greatly valued educated slaves. After leaving Mali, Ibn Battuta passed through the town of Taggada, east of Mali, where he himself purchased a woman slave. During his return journey across the Sahara to Morocco, he informs us that his caravan included six hundred women slaves.

It has already been stated earlier in the description of Mansa Musa's pilgrimage that Mansa Musa's entourage is said to have consisted of a large number of slaves—as many as twelve thousand according to one account. Mansa Musa is also said to have purchased some Turkish slaves in Cairo. One intriguing question regarding Mansa Musa and the slave trade is why he chose to take loans rather than sell some of his slaves when he ran short of funds in Cairo after having returned from Mecca. None of the early sources shed any light on this question. A final point to make about Mansa Musa and slavery is that, according to Kati (1650s), the Malian ruler at a certain point during his reign started the practice of freeing a slave every day (quoted in Fisher & Fisher, 1972).

While we have very limited contemporary source material about slavery in ancient Mali, there is more information available about the institution from the period of the Songhay empire which succeeded ancient Mali and occupied a substantial portion of the territory of ancient Mali. Assuming that there was a good deal of cultural continuity from ancient Mali to Songhay, we can draw some reasonable parallels from the practice of slavery in Songhay and make some general observations. The sources about Songhay inform us that the numbers of slaves were quite large and that a great many of them were war captives. Secondly, the rulers were major owners of slaves. Thirdly, the slaves were used for a variety of social, economic, and political purposes—entertainment, sexual, military, agricultural labor, gift giving, and sometimes for political administration (Hunwick, 1985). Leo Africanus, who traveled through Songhay in the early 1500s, observed that the inhabitants of Timbuktu kept large numbers of men and women slaves. Concerning Gao, the capital of the Songhay empire, Leo Africanus refers to the slave market of the town and witnessed the selling of even young children. An interesting occurrence about the history of slavery in the Songhay empire was the intellectual and legal discourse that took place among several jurists and scholars on such issues as the categories of people who were enslaveable, the rights of slaves, and the emancipation of slaves. Treatises of jurists Ahmed Baba and Al-Maghili are among the most famous and significant such documents related to Muslim slavery in West Africa.

Ralph Austen suggests that between 1100 and 1400, the period that covered the years when ancient Mali was at its peak power and ruled over a substantial part of the Western Sudan, over one and a half million slaves were probably sent across the Sahara from sub-Saharan Africa to North Africa and beyond. However, in the opinion of Levtzion, a larger proportion of slaves was probably exported from states that were located further east from ancient Mali. Levtzion theorizes that for those West African states, such as ancient Ghana, Mali and Songhay, that had large quantities of gold to export, the exports of slaves were of secondary importance for a long period of time (1985).

Slavery and the slave trade increased in importance in the Western Sudan with the passage of time. The expansion of demand for slaves in the Islamic world, the growth in the domestic West African demand, and the development of the Atlantic slave trade all ensured the continuation of slavery well into the modern era. For the Islamic lands in the Middle East, Africa became the most important source of slaves by the nineteenth century, especially after the shutting off of some of the traditional sources of slaves in the Slavic lands and the Russian empire. In the period after the decline of ancient Mali, domestic slavery in the Muslim black African states throughout western Africa increased substantially. Numerous nineteenth century accounts report that in many areas of West Africa, particularly Islamic ones, the slaves constituted a substantial proportion of the total population—as high as three-quarters in some cases (Levtzion, 1985). For excellent detailed analyses and studies of these topics, the readers are referred to the works of Willis, Hunwick, Levtzion, Fisher and others. For our purposes, it is now important to shift the focus to the issues of treatment and occupations of slaves in the Islamic environment beyond the Western Sudan.

Treatment and Occupations of Slaves

While Islam accepted and tolerated the practice of slavery, from the very beginning it also emphasized that the slaves should be treated kindly. Believers are reminded in the Quran and in the *hadith* to be kind to their slaves. Sura 4:36 calls upon the believers to

> Serve Allah and join not any partners with Him: and do good to parents, kinsfolk, orphans, those in need,neighbors who are near, neighbors who are strangers, the companion by your side, the way-farer and what your right hands possess; for Allah loveth not the arrogant, the vainglorious.

The Quran rarely uses the word "slave" in the text. The expression "what your right hands possess" has come to be generally interpreted to include slaves. The most famous *hadith* of the Prophet Muhammad regarding the treatment of slaves states the following:

128

Your slaves are your brethren upon whom Allah has given you authority. So, if one has one's brethren under one's control, one should feed them with the like of what one eats and clothe them with the like of what one wears. You should not overburden them with what they cannot bear, and if you do so, help them (in their hard job).

In other sayings, the Prophet is reported to have warned slave owners not to be cruel, harsh or even discourteous towards their slaves (Lewis, 1980). As Islamic jurisprudence evolved and became more refined through the various schools of law, numerous precise rules dealing with the rights and obligations of the slaves and the masters were formulated. Some of the general rules that affected the slaves were as follows: testimony of a slave was not admissible; slaves could not inherit; they could not enter into business contracts unless specifically authorized; they could not marry without the consent of their masters; women slaves could not have custody of their children fathered by their masters if the masters admitted to their involvement and desired the custody of the children (in such cases the children were considered free and the status of the women slaves was elevated). Some schools of law allowed slaves to own property (at least during a slave's lifetime, after which the property reverted to his master) and to serve as *imams* (prayer leaders) of mosques. It was illegal for masters to separate women slaves from their children by selling mothers and children to separate owners. It was also illegal for a master to cohabit with a slave other than his own or to cohabit with a married slave. It was not permissible for a master to sell a woman slave who had given birth to his child.

The slaves were exempted from performing certain major religious obligations, such as attending the mandatory Friday congregational prayer, fulfilling the duty of pilgrimage or participating in a *jihad*. Slaves were entitled to use part of their labor to earn something for themselves. Masters, on the other hand, were required to provide adequate maintenance and support during old age (Lewis, 1990). According to Lewis, a slave in the Islamic environment "was distinctly better off, in the matter of rights, than a Greek or Roman slave, since Islamic jurists took account of humanitarian considerations." Phillips, in his comparative study of slavery from the Roman period to the beginning of the Atlantic slave trade, concludes that "Muslims seem to have shown considerable humanity towards their slaves" (1985).

Several Europeans who traveled through Islamic countries in the Middle East, North Africa and West Africa during the nineteenth century observed the treatment of slaves firsthand in these countries and recorded their observations, some of which are included here. James Grey Jackson, an Englishman who lived in Morocco for sixteen years in the early 1800s and wrote an account of that country that was published in 1814, stated that "I have known some slaves so attached to their masters from good treatment, that when they have been offered their liberty, they have actually refused it, preferring to continue in servitude." Maj. Gordon Laing observed the following about slaves in the northern Saharan town of Ghadames in the 1820s: they "are treated with so much kindness and have so many privileges that their situation was far superior to that of blacks in the West Indies" (quoted in Porch, 1984). Bernard Lewis in his important work on slavery and Islam concludes that "once they were placed with a family they were reasonably well treated and accepted in some degree as members of the household" (1990, pp. 13-14). Arnold Kemball, a British assistant resident in the Persian Gulf, in a report on the African slave trade dated July 8, 1842, stated the following about the Ethiopian slaves: "Slaves of both sexes are at all times much cared for, well clothed and well fed. The males are early sent to school and having learnt to read and write are employed in the performance of house duties...and very frequently if intelligent in the most trustworthy situations as supercargos of ships, stewards and superintendents. The females are most generally retained as concubines or employed in the lightest duties as attendants in Harems" (quoted in Lewis, 1980). Irwin, who states that "by and large, one can say, it (the life of slaves in the Middle East) was better than in the Americas" suggests two reasons why this was so. According to Irwin, the slave was more valued and relatively more expensive in the Middle East and, secondly, race was not a factor in enslavement (1985).

However, there were many other observers who did not see the picture as being quite so rosy, especially during the capture and the transportation phases of slavery. An eleventh or twelfth century account points out how slaves suffered from hunger and illness as they traveled north across the desert. Captain George Lyon, the first European to travel in the Fezzan region of the Libyan desert, accompanied a slave caravan in 1819 and observed that many women and children slaves died during the journey and that "none of the slave owners ever marched without their whips, which were in constant use" (quoted in Wellard, 1965). Caillie observed during some of his travels in the 1820s that during the crossing of the Sahara Desert, the slaves suffered greatly from thirst and were often savagely punished by their masters. Suffering, certainly, was infinitely greater for those slaves who were castrated and sold as eunuchs, a category of slaves widely used in the Islamic environment as guardians and protectors of the harems. Numerous nineteenth century travelers observed that for every slave who survived the journey to the market three to five suffered death (Fisher & Fisher, 1972).

Once the slaves reached their final destinations they were used for a variety of occupations. We have already described some of the tasks that were performed by the slaves who were retained within the West African Muslim states. Now I will summarize the major uses for which slaves were employed in the wider Islamic world of North Africa and the Middle East. The principal occupations and purposes for which slaves were obtained in these regions were as follows—military, household, sexual, entertainment, deep-sea diving, agricultural, and menial labor. There is some disagreement and debate among scholars as to the economic production role and contribution of slaves in the Islamic world. Lewis suggests that "the Islamic world did not operate on a slave system of production, as is said of classical antiquity....The most important slaves, however, those of whom we have the fullest information, were domestic and commercial, and it is they who were characteristic slaves of the Muslim world" (1990). Willis, on the other hand, suggests that the "slaves of African origin formed a vital thread in the living lines of economic production in the Near and Middle East" (1985). There are several instances where the contribution of African slave labor was unquestionably and significantly linked to economic production. Such cases include the plantation economy of southern Iraq, the salt and copper mines of the Sahara, the date palm groves in the Middle East, and the spice plantations in Eastern Africa. However, slaves seem to have been more widely used in the Islamic world for military, sexual and domestic purposes.

The use of slaves in the military constituted a unique aspect of the culture of slavery in the Islamic world. More than any other civilization, the Muslim world made extensive use of slaves as soldiers and palace guards. Lewis suggests that it was only after the rise of the medieval Islamic state that military slaves became significant. Several Muslim states, particularly medieval Egypt, Ottoman Turkey, Morocco and Arabia, employed large numbers of slaves in their military forces. However, African slaves are said to have been used less frequently for this function. The majority of the military slaves in the Muslim world were obtained from Turkey, Slavic areas and regions bordering Russia. There were some instances in which African slave soldiers were quite important—the Tulunid and Fatimid rulers of Egypt during the ninth and tenth centuries respectively used large numbers of black African slave soldiers; Abd al-Rahman I, the ruler of Cordoba (Spain) in the eighth century; and the rulers of Tunisia between the eighth and the eleventh centuries. There is an interesting case of Sultan Ismail, a ruler of Morocco in the seventeenth century, who chose to reorganize his army in order to employ predominantly African slaves and former slaves. He believed that unlike free men the slaves more strongly exhibited certain qualities—bravery, resoluteness, aptitude and endurance (Batron, 1985). He then decreed the purchase of all legally owned slaves in his territory for service in his military forces. As can be expected in such a culture, the slave soldiers sometimes became so powerful that they overthrew their masters and established themselves as the rulers. The most famous such case—the Mamluks of Egypt—has already been described in an earlier chapter.

It was not unusual for slaves to be employed in the upper echelons of secular and religious administrative structures in some Muslim states. According to Irwin, "It was possible for an African, in the Middle East and India, to reach to the very top of the social and political ladder" (1985). He then suggests that an African once served as the *mufti* (principal religious leader) of Mecca. O'Fahey suggests that slaves were commonly used in such administrative positions "as counterweight to an hereditary or territorial nobility" (1985). The practice of appointing eunuch slaves to state offices is regarded to have been well established in the Muslim states of North Africa. Hiskett cites the case of a West African Habe chief, Mohammad Shashere (1573-82), who seems "to have been dependent upon a court hierarchy or servile origin" (1985).

Sexual slaves were an important feature of the Islamic slave culture, both in the Muslim black African states and in the rest of the Islamic world. Consequently, women slaves were in greater demand in the slave markets of the Muslim world. They constituted the greater proportion of slaves in the trade. Sometimes as many as two-thirds of slaves brought from black Africa and sold in the markets of Egypt were females (Walz, 1985). According to Robertson and Klein, most slaves in nineteenth century Africa south of the Sahara were women. While nearly two-thirds of the slaves purchased by the merchants involved in the Atlantic slave trade were males, the Muslim market and the local African market purchased mostly women and children.

The presence of women in large numbers as victims in the slave system is well documented over an extensive period of time by travelers from Ibn Battuta in the fourteenth century to Heinrich Barth in the nineteenth century. The women slaves, in addition to being used primarily for sexual purposes, were also used as entertainers (primarily as dancers and singers), for domestic chores, and to a lesser degree for economic production. In the markets of the Muslim world, women slaves, along with eunuchs, were generally sold at higher prices. Islam limited the number of wives a man could have to four, but he might have many concubines. Thus, concubinage became a very prominent feature of the Islamic culture. Many Muslim rulers maintained harems consisting of hundreds of concubines. In a very interesting document from the eleventh century, Ibn Butlan provided detailed descriptions and characteristics of women slaves from several different parts of the world—India, Arabia, Berber lands, Yemen, East Africa, Ethiopia, Nubia, Afghanistan, Turkey, Armenia, and Greece (Lewis, 1987). The following excerpt is an example of the kind of information contained in this particular document:

> The Nubian women, of all the black races, have ease and grace and delicacy. Their bodies are dry, while their flesh is tender; they are strong and at the same time slender and firm. The climate of Egypt suits them, since they drink the water of the Nile, but if they are removed to some place other than Egypt, diseases of the blood and acute sicknesses overcome them and pain racks their bodies. Their characters are pure, their appearance attractive, and there is in them religion and goodness, virtue, chastity, and submissiveness to the master, as if they had a natural bent for slavery." (Lewis, 1987)

However, of the African women slaves exported to the Muslim countries, the Ethiopian slaves were in high demand, particularly the younger ones. According to Walz, "there seems to have been a market preference for Ethiopian slaves, who were considered exceptionally handsome and intelligent" (1985). The expansion of the Ottoman power in the Red Sea in the sixteenth century led to a significant increase in the export of Ethiopian slaves to the Ottoman empire, Persia, and India. Along with Ethiopia, the Savannah regions of West Africa, the Sudan, the Horn of Africa and East Africa supplied the bulk of the black African slaves destined for the Muslim world. Concubines, however, were not only maintained by the ruling class. Burton, who visited Mecca in the nineteenth century, observed that most men in Mecca had black concubines.

Among the African male slaves exported to the Muslim world, the eunuchs were generally the most expensive. They were extensively employed in the royal palaces as guardians of the royal wives and the harems and in the households of the nobles and rich merchants. Not only were the eunuchs sold at higher prices, but oftentimes they were sold only in private auctions, and on many occasions they were bought even before reaching the markets. According to Phillips, centers existed along trade routes in Europe, Asia and Africa where castrating procedures were performed (1985). By the nineteenth century, eunuchs were acquired overwhelmingly from Africa and some of the eunuchs came to wield immense power by controlling access to the inner chambers of the royal palaces.

A very interesting dimension to the use of eunuchs in the Islamic world relates to their use in the *Haram*, the sacred precincts of the mosque in Mecca. Eunuch slaves came to be used extensively from the late eighth century for providing care-taking services at the mosque and as police (Peters, 1994a). A 1925 account states that all the eunuchs used at the mosque in Mecca, about fifty in all, were black Africans.

Most major Islamic cities, African and Middle Eastern and beyond, including the Holy City of Mecca, had a slave market. Leo Africanus made brief mention of the slave market of Gao, capital of the Songhay empire. These markets are said to have been "under strict state control in order to protect the buyers from unethical practices" (Talib, 1992). Cairo was a major market for the buying and selling of African slaves from several points of origin. Age, sex, health, physical appearance, shade of skin color, talent and place of origin are among some of the variables that determined the prices of slaves. Burckhardt, who was in Mecca in 1829, described the slave market of Mecca which was known as Suwayqa where Abyssinian (Ethiopian) male and female slaves were sold. The buyers included many pilgrims, and the most attractive slaves were sold for approximately one hundred and twenty dollars (quoted in Peters, 1994a). According to Burton, the buyers in the Holy City got the first pick of the thousands of African slaves that landed in Arabia before they were sent off to Egypt and Turkey.

One aspect of the Muslim culture of slavery that generated controversy in the Muslim world was the enslavement of Muslims by their fellow Muslim brothers. The Islamic *shariah* (religious law) came to strictly forbid this practice. Yet this occurred in several parts of the Muslim world during different time periods. The *shariah* regulations, however, were often ignored. According to Lewis, "the enslavement of free Muslims was totally forbidden...but the practice continued, especially in Africa" (1990). The African ruler Sunni Ali, who initiated the major conquests that led to the establishment of the Songhay empire in the fifteenth century West Africa, accumulated many captive slaves. He did not adhere to the ban against the enslavement of fellow Muslims (Hunwick, 1985). Numerous other similar examples are to be found in the literature. Several Muslim jurists wrote opinions condemning such practices by Muslim traders and rulers. Ahmed Baba's treatise on the subject has already been referred to earlier. Reacting to the continued enslavement of black Africans who were Muslims in Morocco in the nineteenth century, the Moroccan jurist, Al-Nasiri, described such practice as "one of the greatest abominations against religion, because the black people are Muslim people, with the same rights and duties as ourselves" (quoted in Lewis, 1990). According to Lewis, Muslim jurists did not condone the enslavement of free Muslims regardless of their race or origin.

Having discussed many important aspects of the institution of slavery and slave trade in the Islamic world, we now turn our focus to the subject of emancipation and the abolition of slavery and the slave trade in the Islamic world. Slavery has not totally disappeared in the Islamic world. Certain countries, most notably Mauritania and the modern-day Sudan, are often pointed out in the media and in various reports issued by human rights groups as countries where traditional forms of slavery continue to the present day. In these countries, the lighter-skinned Arabs and Berbers are reported to keep in bondage many black Africans, Muslims and Christians.

Emancipation

Manumission of slaves has been an important aspect of the Islamic culture from the very beginning. As pointed out earlier, during the time of the Prophet Muhammad, slaves were granted freedom upon conversion. Islam placed a high value in the emancipation of the slaves even though it did not mandate it. The Quran and the *hadith* recognize manumission as a meritorious and recommended course of action. One of the verses in the Quran says:

> Piety does not consist in turning your face to the
> East or the West. The pious man is one who

believes in Allah and the Last Day, in the Angels, the Scripture, and the Prophets; who gives a portion of his wealth to neighbors, orphans, the poor, travelers, beggars; who frees his slaves; who says his prayers and gives alms; who fulfills the agreements he has contracted; who is patient in adversity, in suffering, and in the moment of danger; such are the believers and the pious. (Sura 2:176)

Another verse (Sura 90:13) states that freeing the bondman is one of the good deeds that a believer can perform to be on the right side.

There are also many *hadith* that encourage the believers to free their slaves. These include "Whoever frees a Muslim slave, Allah will save all parts of his body from the (Hell) fire as he has freed the body-parts of the slave"; "The manumission of the most expensive slave and the most beloved by his master is the best kind of manumission"; "Whoever frees his share of a common slave and has sufficient money to free him completely, should let its price be estimated by a just man and give his partners the price of their shares and manumit the slave"; "He who has a slave-girl and educates and treats her nicely and then manumits and marries her, will get a double reward." Many slaves received their freedom during the life of the Prophet Muhammad.

The Quran offers several incentives to the Muslims to free their slaves. The freeing of a slave is recommended as a way to atone for wrongdoing.

> Never should a believer kill a believer; but (if it so happens) by mistake (compensation is due): if one (so) kills a believer it is ordained that he should free a believing slave and pay compensation to the deceased's family unless they remit it freely....For those who find this beyond their means (is prescribed) a fast for two months running: by way of repentance to Allah: for Allah hath all knowledge and all wisdom. (Sura 58:7)

The Quran also encourages Muslims to allow their slaves to enter into contracts to buy out their freedom.

> And if any of your slaves ask for a deed in writing (to enable them to earn their freedom for certain

sum) give them such deed if ye know any good in them. (Sura 24:33)

Thus in the Islamic tradition freeing of slaves was left as a voluntary and an individual act. How did the Muslims respond to these recommendations of the Quran and the *hadith*? The literature points out many instances in which Muslims, leaders as well as ordinary believers, showed their piety by freeing their slaves. Lewis states that many of the conquered peoples who were enslaved following the conquests were eventually converted to Islam and liberated. It is reported that the second *Caliph* (supreme leader), Umar, when he saw one of his slaves praying, liberated him. Askiya Muhammad of Songhay freed many slaves who claimed that they were Muslims when they had been enslaved by his predecessor, Sunni Ali. When the scholars of Timbuktu were given women slaves as gifts by Sunni Ali, some of these scholars chose to marry them rather than take them as slaves (Hunwick, 1985). There are also instances where slaves were granted contracts to purchase their freedom. Among the Hausa people of West Africa, such occasions are said to have been observed with a ceremony which included the sacrifice of a ram, the shaving of the former slave's head and a new name given to the freed slave. Military slaves are said to have often been freed after certain years of service. Also, jurist could declare slaves emancipated if they were subjected to excessive ill-treatment by their masters.

Concubine women slaves were affected by law and tradition in several different ways in the Islamic slave culture. Those who bore children of their Muslim masters acquired many rights of free persons. The birth of such a child is said to have improved her position. While she did not receive automatic freedom under such a circumstance, it was illegal for her master to sell her, and she received her freedom upon his death. In addition, her child was considered a freeborn individual and was considered as equal to the children born to the master's wife. Many children born to concubine slaves in the Islamic culture are said to have risen to positions of power and prestige. Hunwick states that during the sixteenth and seventeenth centuries, in the case of the famous African Muslim state of Songhay, most of the rulers of the Askiya dynasty were sons of concubines (1985). Will Durant in his multi-volume study of civilizations states, "It is astonishing how many sons of slaves rose to high places in the intellectual and political world of Islam, how many...became kings" (1950). Also, marriages between free Muslims and concubine women slaves were quite common which resulted in the freedom for the women. Most of the *caliphs* of the Abbasid dynasty are said to have been born to slave mothers (Phillips, 1984). The following statement by Lewis is quite telling: "The slave population in the Islamic Middle East was constantly drained by the liberation of slaves—sometimes as an act of piety, most commonly through the recognition and liberation, by a freeman, of his offspring by a slave mother" (1990).

However, the Islamic world did not witness the growth of an abolition movement like the ones that evolved in the Western world. This is so, it is argued, because Muslims did not view slavery as a moral problem. It can safely be stated that it was due to the Western influences and pressures that the Muslim countries began to pass laws banning slavery and slave trade. In the second half of the nineteenth century, rulers of numerous Muslim countries issued decrees of emancipation and signed treaties with the Western powers pledging to take measures to end the slave trade. It is ironic that some of the holiest men of Islam vigorously defended slavery and resisted its discontinuance. Their reasoning has been that whatever is permitted in the Holy Book cannot be disallowed by human legislation. In the 1850s, when Ottoman Turkey banned slave trade, some of the leaders of Mecca declared the Turks to be non-Muslims as a result of their antislavery actions (Peters, 1994a).

It is also rather ironic that some of the Europeans who traveled through some of the Middle Eastern Muslim countries during the nineteenth century argued that slavery in Muslim lands should not be banned because it was benevolent towards the slaves. The Dutchman Snouck Hurgronje, the Englishman J. F. Keane, and the Austrian Ludwig Stross, who all visited Arabia in the 1880s, strongly expressed their opposition to the abolition of slavery in the Muslim lands (Lewis, 1990).

The abolition of slavery and slave trade in the Islamic lands is regarded by some authors to have been the single most important cause for the decline of the trans-Saharan trade by the end of the nineteenth century. The trade, which contributed so much to the historical development of the Western Sudan, is now only a tiny fraction of what it used to be. The end of the slave trade, no doubt, contributed to the decline of the trans-Saharan trade. But other factors also must be considered in its decline—the development of the trans-Atlantic trade, the establishment of a colonial order which resulted in the increased importance of the coastal regions, the political and economic decline of the Islamic world, and the diminished supplies of gold. Lapidus identifies the construction of the railways as a crucial cause for the decline of the trans-Saharan trade. "The railways," according to Lapidus, "destroyed the trans-Saharan traffic and ended the long struggle begun by the Atlantic slave trade, between the Saharan and European peoples, for control of the commerce of Africa. Henceforth international trade would move by rail to the coast rather than by camel across the desert" (1988).

Slavery was an enduring feature of the Islamic world for nearly fourteen centuries. In its practice it had some important differences as compared with Western slavery. However, like the Atlantic slavery, it also greatly affected the peoples of the Western Sudan and Africa in general. In the next section, its impact is summarized.

Impact

Slavery affected both the countries of origin of the slaves and countries of their destination, although in different ways and to different degrees. The most important consequences of slavery were demographic, economic, cultural and political, even though the full impact of slavery will never be known. Although the Islamic slavery is regarded to have been milder than its Atlantic counterpart by many authors, the suffering inflicted upon and experienced by those taken into slavery is difficult to imagine and adequately describe. The kidnappings, mutilations, beatings, forced labor, and forced marches were all characteristics of the Islamic slavery as well. The trans-Saharan trade routes not only carried a multitude of commercial items, but they were also strewn with the skeletal remains of uncountable numbers of captured human beings who perished along the way.

Along with the suffering of the Africans taken into slavery, the loss of population is the second major consequence. Historians disagree on the issue of the magnitude of the export of African slaves to the Islamic lands of North Africa, the Middle East and beyond. Mauny has estimated the figure to be approximately fourteen million. Austen has estimated that seven and a half million slaves were taken across the Sahara Desert between the middle of the seventh and the end of the nineteenth centuries. Other historians are either reluctant to accept such estimates or believe that the numbers were considerably lower. Fage, for instance, states, "It is safer to conclude that, extending over a very much longer period, the trans-Saharan trade removed fewer Negroes than the Atlantic trade, and that its effect on the West African population during the time the Atlantic trade was operating was relatively minor" (1969). July argues that the estimates mentioned above should be regarded as questionable because they are generalized from very limited data (1975). Davis states, "Given the scarcity and unreliability of quantitative evidence, the magnitude of the Islamic slave trade cannot be measured with any precision" (1984). One observation that many Muslim scholars make is that if the number of African slaves taken to the Islamic lands was as high as suggested above, then substantially larger numbers of African descendants of African slaves should be present in the populations of the Islamic countries of the Middle East and North Africa as is the case in the Americas. The absence of large numbers of African descendants in these countries, according to this opinion, suggests that the numbers of slaves taken to these countries were considerably smaller.

As was the case in the Atlantic slavery, the African slaves in the Islamic system became converted to the religion of their masters. Islam gained many more adherents through the slave system even though conversion did not automatically result in emancipation. However, unlike in the Christian world, there was greater integration in religion between the slaves and the masters. It was generally accepted in Islam that in the eyes of Allah all believers were equal. While racial prejudice against darker and black-skinned peoples was certainly found among the lighter-skinned Muslims, religious segregation as such did not develop in the Islamic world. Mosques and other religious institutions were for the benefit of all believers regardless of racial or ethnic origin. Barriers among groups of Muslims were more the result of doctrinaire differences. The Islamic slavery also manifested a greater degree of mixing between the masters and the slaves. Conversions, marriages between masters and slaves, the widely practiced system of concubinage, and a greater acceptance by the masters of children born to their concubine slaves are some of the major factors that facilitated the integration. Many offspring from such relationships rose to positions of political prominence in the Islamic countries as has already been pointed out above. Numerous others have left their mark in the cultural fields—poetry, musical arts, prose and religious sciences (Talib, 1992).

The taking of millions of Africans into slavery certainly had negative consequences for the growth of Africa's economies. Again, the extent of this loss can never be fully calculated. On the other hand, the African slaves contributed substantially to the commercial wealth of many Muslims. In some Islamic areas, their labor was extremely vital for agricultural and mineral production.

Another impact of the Islamic slave system upon Africa was that it ended some of the traditional causes and motives for enslavement that existed among the Africans before their conversion to Islam. Debt, adultery and theft were important reasons for enslavement in the traditional cultures. Islam did not allow enslavement for debt while crimes of adultery and theft were punished according to the *shariah* rules—lashes and sometimes amputations. Also, under Islam the practice of human sacrifices, another cause of frequent enslavement in traditional cultures, was not allowed.

Finally, some authors regard Muslims, particularly Arabs, to have been principally responsible for the massive exploitation of African labor through slave trade because, as argued by Wellard, "it was they who organized the vast traffic in human merchandise out of Africa to the Atlantic and Mediterranean ports" (1965). Another author even blames, though indirectly, the Muslims of the Middle East for the Atlantic slave trade by arguing that since it was they who transmitted the knowledge of the manufacture of sugar to the Europeans during the crusades, they gave rise to the circumstances that led to the large-scale traffic of African slaves across the Atlantic (Phillips, 1985).

CHAPTER VII

DECLINE OF ANCIENT MALI

Introduction

Ancient Mali entered a long period of gradual decline following the death of Mansa Musa in 1337. When Ibn Battuta visited Mali in the 1350s, the empire still seemed to be significantly intact and powerful. But by the end of the fourteenth century, the authority of the central administration had considerably weakened, and the disintegration of the empire, especially in the northern provinces, had set in. Several internal and external causes contributed to the eventual decline of ancient Mali. As an empire of sorts, Mali was a kingdom that had been built up through conquests. A large variety of Sudanese and Sahelian peoples had been brought under the domination of the Malinke. Mali's imperial system, like other imperial systems created through conquests, contained within itself discontented groups of people who awaited opportune moments to break the chains of imperial subjugation and regain their self-determination. Thus, revolts and rebellions on the part of the conquered and subjugated population constituted one major reason for decline. The Songhay people presented ancient Mali with one of the first challenges to its authority and domination.

Another major internal factor contributing to the decline of Mali was the rivalry and contest for power within the ruling dynasty. By the end of the fourteenth century, the contest for power among the descendants of Sundiata, the founder of the empire, had become quite intense and bloody. Mali experienced much civil strife and instability as a result.

The external factors that played a major part in the decline of ancient Mali included attacks upon the state by neighboring peoples and the loss of control over the vital trans-Saharan trade centers. During the fifteenth century ancient Mali came under major attack from the Tuaregs, the Mossi, and the Fulbe peoples. Mali increasingly lost territory and control over important towns to these attackers. The internal and external factors that led to Mali's decline and the related dynamics of this process are explored in detail below.

Dynastic Rivalry

Unwise rulers who ascended to the throne of ancient Mali after Mansa Musa and intra-familial rivalry for power in the latter part of the fourteenth century were two leadership related causes that contributed to the decline of Mali. Ibn Khaldun has. provided us some disturbing descriptions of the quality of some of the Malian rulers who came after Mansa Musa and the struggle for power between different branches of the Sundiata family. We are informed that Mansa Musa was succeeded by his son Mansa Magha, who ruled for four years during the latter part of the 1330s. When Mansa Musa had gone on the pilgrimage, he had left the reins of power in the hands of this son. So it is certain that he had been groomed for power for more than a decade. However, his reign was very short and we do not have much information about this era. Levtzion suggests that in passing the throne to his son, Mansa Musa deprived the throne to his (Mansa Musa's) own brother—Sulayman. Therefore, it is conceivable that Mansa Magha's reign ended after a relatively short span as a result of being forced out of power.

Mansa Magha was succeeded by Mansa Sulayman—Mansa Musa's brother. He is said to have ruled for about twenty-four years. Mali was still the most powerful kingdom in the Western Sudan during his reign. Its military might and economic prosperity were unchallenged in the region. It was during the reign of Mansa Sulayman that Ibn Battuta had traveled to Mali in the 1350s. Ibn Battuta gives quite impressive accounts about the pomp and pageantry surrounding the court of Mansa Sulayman and the wealth displayed at the royal court. However, Ibn Battuta also had some harsh words for the Malian ruler. He described him as a very miserly ruler, based partly upon the fact that he did not lavish expensive gifts upon the North African world traveler. Ibn Battuta remarked that the people of Mali also disliked Mansa Sulayman because he was greedy. Despite these negative characterizations of Mansa Sulayman, and the fact that his regime is said to have experienced and survived a coup attempt, the imperial power of the kingdom was intact. It was after the reign of Mansa Sulayman that matters deteriorated.

Ibn Khaldun informs us that Mansa Sulayman's death was followed by a struggle for power and civil strife. The struggle was basically between the descendants of Mansa Musa and the descendants of Mansa Sulayman. Mansa Sulayman's son, Mansa Qasa, emerged victorious from this conflict. But he was continually challenged by the grandson of Mansa Musa, Mari Jata, and Mansa Qasa's reign lasted only nine months. He was succeeded by Mari Jata, who is said to have ruled for fourteen years. Mansa Musa's grandson seems to have been a far cry from his illustrious grandfather. Ibn Khaldun, based upon information provided to him by a resident of Mali, describes Mansa Mari Jata as a wicked and tyrannical ruler who squandered the wealth of Mali. Mari Jata is said to have squandered so much wealth that he was forced to sell one of the most prized possessions of ancient Mali—a huge nugget of gold which was believed to have been one of the rarest and most precious pieces of gold in existence. He is said to have sold this precious nugget to some Egyptian traders for a relatively small sum. Mansa Mari Jata died in 1374 after having suffered for two years with sleeping sickness.

Mari Jata was succeeded by his son Mansa Musa II who attempted to return the kingdom to a more normal course. He is said to have been a more just ruler, but his principal minister is said to have exercised much control over him. He was succeeded by his brother, who was assassinated after a rule of only about one year. Following him, a usurper, Sandaki, came to the throne and ruled for only a few months until he was assassinated. After Sandaki's reign, the dynastic struggle became even more complicated. It will be recalled that up to the accession of Mansa Musa to the throne of Mali, the rulers were the descendants of Sundiata Keita, the founder of the empire. The succeeding rulers came from the ranks of his sons and grandsons. With Mansa Musa, the line of succession shifted to the descendants of Sundiata Keita's brother. Now, following the death of Mansa Musa II around 1387, a descendant of Sundiata Keita claimed the throne. These internal conflicts towards the end of the fourteenth century led to instability in the realm which prompted subject peoples like the Songhay to secede from the empire and go on their own.

Ascendancy of Songhay

The people and the state of Songhay were located to the north and east of the heartland of ancient Mali. The towns of Gao and Kawkaw formed the nuclei of the country of the Songhay. They were first mentioned in the Arabic sources in the late 900s. The rulers of Kawkaw are believed to have embraced Islam quite early on; they were probably the first in the Western Sudan to convert to Islam as result of the presence and influence of Muslim traders. Archaeological evidence uncovered around Gao suggests that contact may have existed between the Muslim rulers of Gao and Spain (Levtzion, 1976). Gao and Kawkaw had become important links in the trans-Saharan trade between the Western Sudan and North Africa. The importance of the Gao region in the trade network eventually attracted the aggressive attention of the growing kingdom of Mali. Therefore, around the middle of the 1200s, the *Mansas* of Mali extended their domination over the Gao region. Some records suggest that the establishment of Malian control over Gao did not occur until the reign of Mansa Musa in the 1320s. Mansa Musa's army is said to have conquered Gao, and Mansa Musa himself is known to have stopped over in Gao to acknowledge the conquest while he was on his way back from his visit to Egypt and Arabia. In any case, from the 1320s onward, the Songhay people and country were brought under the firm control of the kingdom of Mali.

During the last quarter of the fourteenth century, as Mali experienced dynastic dispute and the resulting chaos (discussed in detail below), the Songhay people of Gao took advantage of the situation to overthrow the control of Mali and consolidate their own independence. In the process of this revolt against the rule of Mali, the Songhay had established the second of their three dynasties, the Sonni dynasty. There are differences of opinion among scholars regarding the timing of the establishment of the Sonni dynasty. However, by the early 1400s, the Sonni dynasty was well established, its rulers had successfully consolidated their independence from Mali, and they had embarked on building their own empire. The expansion of Songhay first occurred primarily at the expense of ancient Mali. The Sonni rulers Mohammad Dao and Sulayman Dandi conquered and annexed a number of Malian provinces. They are even said to have sacked the Malian capital of Niani in the early 1400s. This would have represented quite a bold and deep penetration into Mali. It was Sonni Ali Ber, who came to power in 1464 and ruled until 1492, who dealt the final blows to the power of Mali in the northern region of the Sahel. These northern Sahelian provinces were now lost to Mali. Sonni Ali Ber and Askiya Mohammad Toure (1493-1528), the founder of the third Songhay dynasty, transformed Songhay into the largest medieval empire of the Western Sudan. At the same time that the Songhay started their ascendancy, another group of subject people also took advantage of Mali's weakness and assaulted its power in the northern and northwestern portions of the empire. These were the Tuaregs.

Tuareg Attacks

The Tuaregs are a major group of Berber people. They are said to have occupied many areas of northern Africa, especially the massifs of the Sahara, for nearly two thousand years. The Tuareg culture has been characterized by a pastoralist lifestyle; well-defined class structure-nobles, vassals, and slaves; and organization of tribal confederacies. They had also become an important factor in the trans-Saharan trade by controlling some of the trade routes and transportation services. Their presence was significant in many of the trans-Saharan termini in the Western Sudan such as Walata, Audaghost, Timbuktu, Tuat and others. Many of these Tuaregs who had been brought under the control of the powerful Mansas of Mali had become sedentary and quite engaged in the commercial life of ancient Mali. Others had remained nomadic and rebellious to the authority of Mali.

As the ruling dynasty of Mali became beset with intense dynastic conflicts after 1380s, the Tuaregs, like the Songhay, agitated for greater autonomy and self-determination. In the early 1400s, under their leader Akil Ag Melaoul, their challenges to the Malian authority became bolder and more frequent. They gained control of some of the most important towns in Mali, such as Walata and Timbuktu, in the 1430s. Timbuktu was first founded by Tuaregs in the 1100s, but it began to emerge as an important town during the control of Mali. The loss of these major market towns, along with the loss of Gao and Kawkaw to the Songhay, resulted in significant economic, military and psychological setbacks for the kingdom of Mali. The Tuaregs themselves, however, were not able to retain control over these towns for too long. After about thirty years, they in turn were overwhelmed by the Songhay, who, in the 1460s, under their conquering king Sonni Ali, occupied Timbuktu, Jenne and many other territories formerly belonging to ancient Mali. However, the Tuareg interlude was not entirely negative for the town of Timbuktu. The sedentary Tuaregs provided the ranks of jurists, scholars and Islamic theologians whose works eventually contributed to Timbuktu's widespread fame as a major center of learning.

Also, in the fifteenth century, Mali came under the attacks of the Mossi and Fula peoples as these groups were undergoing their own expansion through the Western Sudan. Although Mali had lost a substantial portion of its territory during the fifteenth century, it was still regarded as a rich kingdom. Leo Africanus, who visited the capital of Mali in the early 1500s, observed that Mali was a land rich in agriculture, artisans and merchants. In

Mali, according to Leo Africanus, there were many temples, priests and scholars.

The Last Mansas

The loss of the northern and eastern territories of the empire to the Songhay and other attackers, needless to say, had considerably lessened the size of the empire. Nevertheless, Mali continued to rule over many lands along the upper Niger River, and its rule also extended towards the Atlantic coast. In addition, numerous territories along the Gambia and Senegal Rivers were subject to Mali's rule all through the sixteenth century.

From the middle of the 1400s, a new external power had entered the West African scene—the Europeans, principally the Portuguese. The Portuguese were the pioneers in Europe's exploration of the African coastline. We have scant but helpful references in the journals of these early Portuguese explorers regarding Mali. The accounts of several of these European explorers—Alvise Cadamosto, Diogo Gomes, Duarte Pacheco Pereira, and Alvares d'Almeida—inform us that Mali was not only still well-known in the 1500s, but also that several coastal states were subjects of and paid allegiance to Mali. From these accounts we learn that Mali still controlled the gold-producing region of Bure in the 1500s and that its trade had shifted from trans-Saharan to trans-Atlantic. New trading towns such as Sutuco and Jagrancura had taken the place of the Saharan towns as entrepots for many Malian merchants. The gold-salt trade was still quite important. Cadamosto, who journeyed to West Africa in the 1450s, observed that the coastal West Africans informed him that great quantities of salt were mined at Taghaza (visited by Ibn Battuta in the 1350s) and transported to Mali where they were sold very quickly at high price. Cadamosto also informs us that "silent trade" or "dumb barter" (discussed in detail in an earlier chapter) was still a common practice. "In this way," he stated, "they carry on their trade without seeing or speaking to each other. Although it is difficult to believe this, I can testify that I have had this information from many merchants, Arab as well as Azanaghi, and also from persons in whom faith can be placed" (Crone, 1937).

The gold trade remained an important commodity for Malian traders all though the 1400s and 1500s. It is said that frequently the Malian traders brought so much gold to the coastal trading centers that they could not dispose all of it in their transactions. Diego Gomes, who visited the interior market town of

Cantor along the Senegal River in the 1450s, observed the following:

> I questioned the negroes at Cantor as to the road which led to the countries where there was gold, and asked who were the lords of that country. They told me that the king's name was Bormelli, and that the whole land of the negroes on the right side of the river was under his dominion....They said further that he was the lord of all the mines, and that he had before the door of his palace a mass of gold just as it was taken from the earth, so large that twenty men could scarcely move it, and that the king always fastened his horse to it, and kept it as curiosity on account of its being found just as it was, and its great size and purity. (Crone, 1937)

The Malian merchants, known as Wangaras, also ventured more to the forest lands of the south and, in the process, contributed significantly to the expansion of Islamic culture through West Africa.

There were also official Portuguese representatives who traveled to the court of Mali. Barros informs us that the Portuguese King Joao sent a delegation as early as the 1480s to the interior of West Africa, including to "Mandi Mansa, one of the most powerful of that part of the Province of Mandinga" (Crone, 1937). One such delegation is said to have been received by Mansa Mahmud III in the 1530s (Ly Tall, 1984). Unfortunately, not many details about these diplomatic contacts are available.

However, as the sixteenth century marched on, other dynamics—expansion of European influence, the growth of the trans-Atlantic slave trade, rise of new states—added pressure upon the kingdom of Mali until it vanished as a major power. In its waning years, ancient Mali is said to have sought the help of the Portuguese in its efforts to ensure its continued existence in the face of attacks from other expanding states such as the Bambara. But help did not come, and by the end of the century, Mali was fragmented, and parts of it became absorbed by other African states.

Very few details are available about the last of the Mansas. It will be recalled that at the end of the 1300s, as a result of the dynastic disputes and civil strife, the descendants of Sundiata Keita had regained the throne of Mali. Mansa Uli, Mansa Mahmud II, Mansa Mahmud III, and Mansa Mahmud IV are the four rulers of

Mali during the 1500s that are referenced to in the accounts. It was Mansa Mahmud III, who, in the 1530s, is said to have received the Portuguese delegation led by Joao de Barros to discuss issues involving trade along the Gambia River. Mansa Mahmud IV attempted in the 1590s to reconquer the city of Jenne but failed (Ly Tall, 1984). With this failure, the decline of Mali was almost complete. As-Sadi in *Tarikh as-Sudan* makes a fairly harsh observation about the decline of Mali. He stated, "The people of Mali were very powerful and their strength passed all limits....Their oppression, arrogance and excess at the end of the dynasty caused Allah to destroy them by His punishment" (quoted in Levtzion, 1980). Thus ends the story of what Saad describes as "the greatest geopolitical formation in the history of West Africa" (Saad, 1983).

The present-day country of Mali has become the cultural heir to a series of most important empires of medieval Africa. A good portion of the territories of ancient Ghana, Mali and Songhay are contained within the boundaries of modern Mali along with many of the population groups associated with these ancient states—the Soninke, Malinke, Tuareg, and Songhay. During the last decade, ethnic tensions were quite high among these groups which resulted in frequent outbreaks of violence. The important cities of Timbuktu, Gao, and Jenne are still in existence and are all within present-day Mali. Unfortunately, they do not enjoy the economic prosperity that they once did, but they continue to enjoy widespread fame and attention for their historical importance. Gold is still mined but in much smaller quantities. Overall, Mali is among the poorest countries of the world economically with a per capita income of about $300 per annum. The Sundiata epic has gained great fame, and some scholars place it in the same category as the other great epics of the world such as *Gilgamesh,* the *Odyssey* and others.

A major challenge confronted by the Government of Mali today is the issue of the pilfering of the antiquities associated with the early cultures of the Western Sudan. This issue has been prominently discussed in several respected journals under such headlines as "The Rape of Mali" (*Archaeology*), "The Loss of Cultural Heritage in Mali" (*African Arts*), "Looting the Antiquities of Mali" (*Antiquity*), and "The Pillage of Archaeological Sites in Mali" (*African Arts*). "Not since the wholesale rape of Egypt's archaeological treasures in the first half of the nineteenth century," according to one source, "has a country been so methodically stripped of its national heritage" (Brent, 1994). Private collectors and museums in the West who pay high prices for artifacts smuggled out of Mali are said to be the primary culprits in fueling this crisis despite the fact that international covenant and national laws of several countries ban the importation of these objects. One can only hope that Malians will be successful in their efforts to protect and preserve the rich legacy of their historical experiences for the future generations.

APPENDIX I: WORKSHEETS

CHAPTER I

1. Explain the factors that contributed to the rise and expansion of ancient Mali.

2. Explain the essential highlights of the Sundiata story and point out some of the key differences in the versions of the story.

3. Discuss the nature of the earliest written sources about ancient Mali—the authors, the sources of their information, and the type of information they provide.

4. Describe the ethnic and geographic dimensions of ancient Mali.

CHAPTER II

1. Discuss the following statement: The Sahara Desert was a bridge rather than a barrier between the Western Sudan and North Africa and beyond.

2. Explain how the trans-Saharan trade contributed to the glory of ancient Mali.

3. The trans-Saharan trade has often been referred to as "silent trade" or "dumb barter." Explain the significance of these terms.

4. What lessons do we learn from the writers who have left accounts of crossing the desert?

CHAPTER III

1. Explain the origin of Islam and when and how Islam expanded to the Western Sudan.

2. Explain when and how Islam expanded to ancient Mali.

3. Explain the economic and political impact of Islam upon ancient Mali.

4. Explain the cultural impact of Islam upon the Western Sudan and ancient Mali.

CHAPTER IV

1. Trace the place of Mansa Musa among the rulers of ancient Mali and explain the circumstances of his ascension to power.

2. Discuss the accomplishments of Mansa Musa and the nature of his rule.

3. What is the controversy about the capital city of ancient Mali?

4. How did Ibn Battuta describe conditions in Mali?

CHAPTER V

1. Explain the significance and the rituals associated with the Islamic pilgrimage.

2. What specific details do the early sources provide us about Mansa Musa's journey to and from Mecca?

3. Identify and describe the specific early sources that provide us details about Mansa Musa's pilgrimage.

CHAPTER VI

1. How did Islam view and deal with the institution of slavery?

2. What do the sources inform us about the existence and the nature of the slave trade and slavery in the Western Sudan and ancient Mali?

3. Analyze the impact of the trans-Saharan slave trade upon the Western Sudan.

4. Explain how the abolition of slave trade and emancipation of slaves occurred in the Islamic regions.

CHAPTER VII

1. Explain the causes and consequences of dynastic rivalry that affected ancient Mali.

2. How did the empire of Songhay and the Tuareg tribes contribute to the decline of ancient Mali?

3. Identify the last Mansas of Mali and explain how
    circumstances had changed for Mali.

4. In your opinion, what is the importance of ancient Mali for
    contemporary Africa?

APPENDIX II: PHOTOS

A camel caravan at rest in the Sahara Desert near Timbuktu

A local market in Timbuktu

A view of houses in Timbuktu

The main street in Timbuktu

Salt market along the Niger River

A local market in Jenne

BIBLIOGRAPHY

Ade Ajayi, J. F., and Michael Crowder, eds. *History of West Africa*. 2nd edition. 2 vols. New York: Columbia University Press, 1976.

Andah, B. Wai. "West Africa Before the Seventh Century." In *General History of Africa*, edited by G. Mokhtar. Berkeley: University of California Press, 1981.

As-Sadi, Abderahman. *Tarikh as-Sudan*. Translated by O. Houdas. Paris: Adrien-Maisonneuve, 1964.

Bagrow, Leo. *History of Cartography*. Revised and enlarged by R. A. Skelton. Cambridge: Harvard University Press, 1964.

Barbour, Nevill. *Morocco*. New York: Walker and Company, 1966.

Barth, Heinrich. *Travels and Discoveries in North and Central Africa*. 3 vols. London: Frank Cass and Company Limited, 1965.

Batran, Aziz Abdalla. "The 'Ulama' of Fas, Mulay Isma'il, and the Issue of Haratin of Fas." In *Slaves and Slavery in Muslim Africa*, edited by John Ralph Willis, vol II. London: Frank Cass and Company Limited, 1985.

Bertol, Roland. *Sundiata: The Epic of the Lion King*. New York: Thomas Y. Crowell Company, 1970.

Blake, John William, translator and editor. *Europeans in West Africa, 1450-1560*. London: The Hakluyt Society, 1942.

Blake, W. O. *The History of Slavery and the Slave Trade*. Columbus, Ohio: J. & H. Miller, 1858.

Bovill, E. W. *The Golden Trade of the Moors*. 2nd ed. Oxford: Oxford University Press, 1970.

Brett, Michael. "Ifriqiya as a Market for Saharan Trade from Tenth to Twelfth Century A.D." *Journal of African History* (10:3), 1969.

Burton, Richard F. *Personal Narrative of a Pilgrimage to El-Medinah and Meccah.* New York: G. P. Putnam & Company, 1856.

Chu, Daniel, and Elliott Skinner. *A Glorious Age in Africa: The Story of Three Great African Empires.* Garden City, N.Y.: Zenith Books, 1965.

Cissoko, Sekene Mody. *Tombouctou et l'Empire Songhay.* Dakar, Senegal: Les Nouvelles Editions Africaines, 1975.

Conrad, David C. "Islam in the Oral Traditions of Mali: Bilali and Surakarta." *Journal of Africa History* (26), 1985.

_____. "A Town Called Dakajalan: The Sunjata Tradition and the Question of Ancient Mali's Capital." *Journal of African History* (35), 1994.

Crone, G. R., translator and editor. *The Voyages of Cadamosto.* London: The Hakluyt Society, 1937.

Davidson, Basil. *Africa: History of a Continent.* New York: Macmillan Company, 1972.

_____. *African Kingdoms.* New York: Time-Life Books, 1971.

_____. *A History of West Africa 1000-1800.* London: Longmans, Green and Company Ltd., 1965.

Davis, David Brion. *Slavery and Human Progress.* New York: Oxford University Press, 1984.

Devisse, J. "Africa in Inter-Continental Relations." In *General History of Africa,* edited by D. T. Niane, vol. IV. Berkeley: University of California Press, 1984.

Dubois, Felix. *Timbuctoo the Mysterious.* Translated from the French by Diana White. N.Y.: Longmans, Green and Co., 1896.

Durant, Will. *The Story of Civilization.* Vol. IV. New York: Simon and Schuster, 1950.

The Encyclopedia of Islam. Leiden: E. J. Brill.

Fage, J. D. "Slavery and the Slave Trade in the Context of West African History." *Journal of African History* (10: 3), 1969.

_____. *A History of West Africa: An Introductory Survey.* Cambridge: Cambridge University Press, 1969.

Fisher, Alan G. B., and Humphrey J. Fisher. *Slavery and Muslim Society in Africa*. Garden City, N.Y.: Doubleday & Company, Inc., 1972.

Fisher, Humphrey. "The Western and Central Sudan and East Africa." In *The Cambridge History of Islam*, edited by P. M. Holt, Ann K. S. Lambton, and Bernard Lewis, vol. 2. Cambridge: Cambridge University Press, 1970.

Garraty, John A., and Peter Gay. *The Columbia History of the World*. N.Y.: Harper & Row, 1972.

Gautier, Emile Felix. *Sahara: The Great Desert*. N.Y.: Octagon Books, 1970.

Guellouz, Ezzedine. *Mecca: The Muslim Pilgrimage*. N.Y.: Paddington Press, Ltd., 1979.

Herodotus, *The Histories*. Translated by George Rawlinson. London: J. M. Dent & Sons Ltd., 1992.

Hiskett, Mervyn. "The Image of Slaves in Hausa Literature." In *Slaves and Slavery in Muslim Africa*, edited by John Ralph Willis. London: Frank Cass and Company Limited, 1985.

Hopkins, A. G. *An Economic History of West Africa*. N.Y.: Columbia University Press, 1973.

Hrbek, I., and M. El Fasi. "Stages in the Development of Islam and Its Dissemination in Africa." In *General History of Africa*, edited by I. Hrbek, abridged edition. Berkeley: University of California Press, 1992.

Hunwick, J. O. "Notes on Slavery in the Songhay Empire." In *Slaves and Slavery in Muslim Africa*, edited by John Ralph Willis, vol. II. London: Frank Cass and Company Limited, 1985.

_____. "The Mid-Fourteenth Century Capital of Mali." *Journal of African History* (14:2), 1973.

Ibn Battuta. *Travels in Asia and Africa 1325-1354*. Translated and selected by H. A. R. Gibb. N.Y.: Augustus M. Kelley, 1969.

Imperato, Pascal James. *Historical Dictionary of Mali*. Metuchen, New Jersey: The Scarecrow Press, Inc., 1977.

Jackson, James Grey. *An Account of the Empire of Morocco and the Districts of Suse and Tafilet*. 3rd ed. London: Frank Cass and Company Limited, 1968.

Johnson, John William. *The Epic of Son-Jara: A West African Tradition*. Bloomington: Indiana University Press, 1992.

July, Robert. *Pre-Colonial Africa: An Economic and Political History*. N. Y.: Charles Scribner's Sons, 1975.

Keenan, Jeremy. *The Tuareg: People of Ahaggar*. N.Y.: St. Martin's Press, 1977.

Killingray, David. *A Plague of Europeans: Westerners in Africa Since the Fifteenth Century*. Baltimore: Penguin Education, 1973.

Ki-Zerbo, Joseph. *Histoire de l'Afrique Noire*. Paris: Hatier, 1978.

Lapidus, Ira M. *A History of Islamic Societies*. N.Y.: Cambridge University Press, 1988.

Le Tourneau, Roger. "North Africa to the Sixteenth Century." In *The Cambridge History of Islam*, edited by P. M. Holt et al. Cambridge: Cambridge University Press, 1970.

Leo Africanus. *The History and Description of Africa and of the Notable Therein Contained*. Translated into English in the Year 1600 by John Pory. Now Edited by Dr. Robert   Brown. 3 vols. N.Y.: Burt Franklin Publisher, 1896.

Levtzion, Nehemiah. "Slavery and Islamization in Africa: A Comparative Study." In *Slaves and Slavery in Muslim Africa*, edited by John Ralph Willis, vol. I. London: Frank Cass and Company Limited, 1985.

_____. *Ancient Ghana and Mali*. N.Y.: African Publishing Company, 1980.

_____. "The Thirteenth- and Fourteenth-Century Kings of Mali." *Journal of African History* (4:3), 1963.

Levtzion, Nehemiah, and J. F. P. Hopkins, eds. *Corpus of Early Arabic Sources for West African History*. Cambridge: Cambridge University Press, 1981.

Lewis, Bernard, ed. *Islam: From the Prophet Muhammad to the Capture of Constantinople*. Vol. II. N.Y.: Oxford University Press, 1987.

_____. *Race and Slavery in the Middle East: An Historical Inquiry.* N.Y.: Oxford University Press, 1990.

Lhote, Henri. "The Fertile Sahara: Men, Animals and the Art of a Lost World." In *Vanished Civilizations of the Ancient World,* edited by Edward Bacon. N.Y.: McGraw-Hill, 1963.

Long, David Edwin. *The Hajj Today: A Survey of the Contemporary Makkah Pilgrimage.* Albany, N.Y.: State University of New York Press, 1979.

Ly Tall, Madina. *L'Empire du Mali.* Dakar, Senegal: Les Nouvelles Editions Africaines, 1977.

_____. "The Decline of the Mali Empire." In *General History of Africa,* edited by D. T. Niane, vol. IV. Berkeley: University of California Press, 1984.

Mahjoubi, A. "The Roman and Post-Roman Period." In *General History of Africa*, edited by G. Mokhtar, vol. II. Berkeley: California University Press, 1981.

Mansfield, Peter. *The Arabs.* N.Y.: Penguin Books, 1980.

Meillassoux, Claude. "L'Itineraire d'Ibn Battuta de Walata a Malli." *Journal of African History* (13:3), 1972.

Meltzer, Milton. *Slavery: A World History.* Updated edition. N.Y.: Da Capa Press, Inc., 1963.

Mohamed, Mamdou N. *Hajj and Umra: From A to Z.* Beltsville, Md.: Amana Publications. 1996.

Muir, William. *The Mamluke or Slave Dynasty of Egypt, A.D. 1260-1517.* Amsterdam: Oriental Press, 1968.

Newberry, C. W. "North African and Western Sudan Trade in the Nineteenth Century: A Re-evaluation." *Journal of African History* (2), 1966.

Niane, D. T. "Relationships and Exchanges among Different Regions." In *General History of Africa*, edited by D. T. Niane, vol. IV. Berkeley: California University Press, 1984.

_____. *Sundiata: An Epic of Old Mali.* Translated by G. D. Picket. London: Longman, 1965.

O'Fahey, R. S. "Slavery and Society in Darfur." In *Slaves and Slavery in Muslim Africa,* edited by John Ralph Willis, vol. II. London: Frank Cass and Company Limited, 1985.

Peters, F. E. *The Hajj: The Muslim Pilgrimage to Mecca and the Holy Places*. Princeton: Princeton University Press, 1944a.

_____. *Mecca: A Literary History of the Muslim Holy Land*. Princeton: Princeton University Press, 1994b.

Phillips, William D., Jr. *Slavery from Roman Times to the Early Transatlantic Trade*. Minneapolis, Minn.: University of Minnesota Press, 1985.

Porch, Douglas. *The Conquest of the Sahara*. N.Y.: Alfred A. Knopf, 1984.

Rashid, Runoko. "Commentary: Black Bondage in Asia." In *African Presence in Asia*, edited by Ivan Van Sertima. New Brunswick, New Jersey: Transaction Books, 1985.

Ritchie, Carson I. A. *Rock Art of Africa*. Philadelphia, Pa.: The Art Alliance Press, 1979.

Robertson, Claire C., and Martin A. Klein, eds. *Women and Slavery in Africa*. Madison, Wisconsin: The University of Wisconsin Press, 1983.

Ross, Michael. *Cross the Desert*. N.Y.: Gordon & Cremonesi Publishers, 1977.

Saad, Elias N. *Social History of Timbuktu: The Role of Muslim Scholars and Notables 1400-1900*. N.Y.: Cambridge University Press, 1983.

Salama, P. "The Sahara in Classical Antiquity." In *General History of Africa*, edited by G. Mokhtar, vol. II. Berkeley: California University Press, 1981.

Savage, E. "Berbers and Blacks: Ibadi Slave Traffic in Eighth-Century North Africa." *Journal of African History* (33), 1992.

Shinnie, Margaret. *Ancient African Kingdoms*. N.Y.: The New American Library, 1965.

Smith, Robert. "Peace and Palaver: International Relations in Pre-colonial West Africa." *Journal of African History* (14:4), 1973.

Snowden, Frank, Jr. *Blacks in Antiquity*. Cambridge, Mass.: Harvard University Press, 1970.

Swift, Jeremy. *The Sahara*. Nederland: Time-Life International, 1975.

Talib, Y. A. "The African Diaspora in Asia." In *General History of Africa*, edited by I. Hrbek, abridged edition, vol. III. Berkeley: California University Press, 1992.

Trimingham, J. Spenser. *A History of Islam in West Africa*. Oxford: Oxford University Press, 1962.

Tucker, Compton J., Harold E. Dregne, and Wilbur W. Newcomb. "Expansion and Contraction of the Sahara Desert from 1980 to 1990." In *Selected Papers on Optical Remote Sensing Theory and Measurements*, edited by James E. Smith. Bellingham, Washington: SPIE Optical Engineering Press, 1977.

Walz, Terrence. "Black Slavery in Egypt During the Nineteenth Century as Reflected in the Mahkama Archives of Cairo." In *Slaves and Slavery in Muslim Africa,* edited by John Ralph Willis. London: Frank Cass and Company Limited, 1985.

Warmington, B. H. "The Carthaginian Period." In *General History of Africa*, edited by G. Mokhtar, vol. II. Berkeley: California University Press, 1981.

Wellard, James. *The Great Sahara*. N.Y.: E. P. Dutton & Co., Inc., 1965.

Willis, John Ralph. "Introduction: The Ideology of Enslavement in Islam." In *Slaves and Slavery in Muslim Africa*, edited by John Ralph Willis, vol. I. London: Frank Cass and Company Limited, 1985.